ONE MORE JULY

BOOKS BY GEORGE PLIMPTON

George Plimpton

ONE MORE JULY

A FOOTBALL DIALOGUE
WITH BILL CURRY

HARPER & ROW, PUBLISHERS
NEW YORK, HAGERSTOWN, SAN FRANCISCO, LONDON

FIRST EDITION

Designed by Gloria Adelson

Library of Congress Cataloging in Publication Data

Plimpton, George.
   One more July.

   1. Curry, Bill, 1942– 2. Football players—
United States—Biography. 3. Football. I. Title.
GV939.C87P55 1977   796.33′2′0924 [B]   76–26247
ISBN 0–06–013376–7

77 78 79 80 10 9 8 7 6 5 4 3 2 1

for Carolyn Curry

"I love it, God help me, I do love it so. . . ."
—General George Patton,
on surveying a battlefield

ONE MORE JULY

Chapter 1

HE PICKED ME UP at the airport in Louisville, Kentucky. I saw
him immediately, standing beyond the people waiting behind
the gate, big-framed, his bare arms crossed; we walked out to
the parking lot. There was barely enough room for my bag in
his car. The back seat of his burgundy-colored Volvo was
packed with effects; a child's Snoopy doll was lying on its back
on the rear window sill, its nose aloft, the property of one of his
two children, who were due in Green Bay with his wife, Carolyn, a couple of weeks into the training season.

I had met Bill Curry three or four years before when I was
up to some participatory journalism with the Baltimore Colts.
He played center, first for the Green Bay Packers, then as All-
Pro with the Colts during his best seasons, but what I remembered him for—besides his kindness in helping me through my
travail as a last-string quarterback—was the considerable study
he gave his own profession: he was one of the few players in the
cliquish training-camp community who made a point of moving

around and sitting at a different table during every meal as if to check out his constituency and his relationship to it. Perhaps he did this to serve some function of self-appraisal; I never asked. He behaved like an excellent reporter on a long assignment. But he was very giving of what he learned, a fine storyteller, and after a while, because he saw how interested I was in what he absorbed, I began to think of him almost as a collaborator.

Since that time he had wandered around the league. The Colts had gone through convulsive changes under their new general manager, Joe Thomas, and Curry, though a team leader, had been traded first to the Houston Oilers—the hope of the management there that he could instill more confident ways within that ineffectual group. Then, after suffering a fearsome leg injury, he was brought to Los Angeles by his former owner in the Baltimore Colt days, Carroll Rosenbloom. And now, the following year, Bart Starr, his old quarterback at Green Bay, newly appointed the club's head coach, had persuaded him to give it one more try with the Packers . . . returning him full circle, ten years later, to the place where he had started.

The injury was what worried him most. He was wearing shorts and as he got behind the wheel of the Volvo I could see the long curved scar, white and new, crossing his kneecap. I asked him how he felt. He said that the knee wasn't bothering him as much as a hamstring problem. But he had been running. In fact, he told me as we drove out of the parking lot, that morning he'd had a couple of hours to spare before my plane was due (he had left Atlanta, his home town, very early), and just for the fun of it he had stopped the Volvo on the Kentucky-Tennessee state line and run back and forth between the two states just so he could say that he'd done it. He ran on the expressway, past a small farm with a woman out digging in the yard. When he ran by for the fourth time, she stood up and, somewhat nervous now, watched him go by. He wanted to reassure her, but he decided she would be utterly undone to see him coming for her, and before he could explain she would be in the house, shouting into a phone for the police. Besides, he didn't have time. He had to keep running.

I had arranged to meet him in Louisville to continue on with him to Green Bay—tagging along to listen, and to keep him company. Certainly the dramatic implications of the trip were evident enough, a veteran going back for one last crack at it. I brought along a tape recorder. As we drove north through the July heat it would pass the time to prod him a bit about that decade of his in professional football, which had started in 1963 when he was drafted the last person by the Packers and the third last in the entire National Football League.

"The *last* person? I hadn't realized that," I said.

We gossiped for a while about the last man in the league drafted by the Baltimore Colts the training season I was there —Don Nottingham, the "Human Bowling Ball," a squattish full-back from Kent State who had an odd, high voice, like an upper-register sigh from an exhausted calliope . . . and who, to every-one's surprise, had gone on to be an excellent addition to the team. The coaches had begun to notice him for his energy on the special teams—the way he led the kickoff down the field, as if the football was an escaped object which it was imperative to retrieve.

"Was there very much interest in you at the start, Bill?" I asked.

"Well, there was," Curry replied. "But not for the same rea-son. It began before I ever got a chance to perform on a special team. My last college game was against the University of Georgia, a game that we lost in the mud. Red Cochran, a Packer coach, rushed out and practically lifted me up off the last pileup."

"What on earth for?" I asked.

"Well, he had been assigned by the Packers to make sure that the rival American Football League didn't get their clutches on

3

me," Curry explained. "I had also been drafted by the Oakland Raiders—number twenty-three out of twenty-three designation! I'll guarantee you I was not the hottest property in *that* year's college crop!

"But Cochran was there—a 'hand-holder' was what the term was. His duty was to stay close by until I had signed a contract with the Packers, and that made me feel wanted. So was the fact that when he took my wife, Carolyn, and me to Dallas the next morning to watch the Packers play—the first time I would see Green Bay in person—we heard that Oakland guy was moseying around the motel. It was all very exciting. Not only did I feel wanted, but I felt I was about to get very wealthy.

"The Packers had just thrashed the Cowboys that afternoon. The Cowboys were a poor team back then, just running up and down the field, and the Packers *crushed* them! With about five minutes left in the game, Pat Peppler, who was the personnel director for the Packers then, took me down on the field and sat me on the end of the bench right by Paul Hornung. Honest to goodness, it was like sitting next to George Washington or something. I could hardly believe where I was. I watched Lombardi close to for the first time. The score was 45 to 10, or something, and he was still dissatisfied. After the game, there was a ten-minute delay before we were allowed in the locker room; everyone in there was looking sullen. It turned out Lombardi had really chewed them out. Terrible offensive performance, in his view. The defense had scored two or three touchdowns, but the offense had been stopped at the goal line a couple of times . . . and he was just *furious.* I was taken around and introduced to Bart Starr. He was very cool. It turned out that he had been chastised just before I got in the room."

"That should have given you some sort of presentiment of what you were getting into," I suggested.

Curry rolled his eyes. "Well, apparently it didn't register, because I ended up signing a contract that night. Financially, it was certainly the most foolish thing I could have done. The

AFL and NFL were just beginning their bidding war. They were willing to pay big money, but nobody realized it yet . . . except Joe Namath, who had been drafted that same year by the Jets and the St. Louis Cardinals. Joe was smart enough to wait a month or so, and then he got the big money; the people who waited along with him realized that there was tremendous competition for their services.

"Well, I had signed by that time. I had asked a sportswriter in Atlanta what was a good signing price. He thought about it and said, 'Gee, if you get a $12,000 salary and a $12,000 bonus, that'll be more than any lineman ever got who came out of Georgia Tech." Which was true. That night back in the motel, I tried to be cagey. I wouldn't say anything—not even a hint of a sum—to either the Packer or the Oakland guys. We just went back and forth for hours until it was two in the morning. All this time Pat Peppler was trying to tell me something. He said, 'Look, I just talked to the old man. I asked him what I could pay you and his response was: "Sign him!" ' I think what Pat was trying to tell me was that Lombardi really wanted me and I could ask for a considerable amount of money. Finally, about two in the morning, I broke down and said what it was I wanted. It seemed like *so* much money. I didn't know if they would laugh at me, or tell me they weren't interested, or what. I finally said, 'I'd like a $12,000 salary and a $12,000 bonus.'

"Pat Peppler sort of smiled. He said, 'I'll tell you what. Suppose we make it twelve five and twelve five.' A thousand dollars more than I'd asked for. I thought I had struck gold! I went running down to the room where Carolyn was asleep and I woke her up. I think we both cried. I was so proud.

"Then back at Georgia Tech I ran into Dave Simmons, who played next to me on defense. We were both linebackers. He had signed with the St. Louis Cardinals, who had drafted him along with Buffalo, and the two clubs had competed back and forth. He was a pretty good linebacker. We were fairly equal. But he had signed for twenty and twenty, *plus* a new automobile. He got literally twice as much as I did . . . though, as a matter of fact, it turned out he never made it in the National Football League. I was just . . . I was *crushed.* Two or three times I actually picked up the phone to call Lombardi, and dialed the number, but then I hung up."

"What would have happened if you'd reached him?" I asked.

"Oh, I had a sense of what would have happened just from those first glimpses of him along the sidelines. He would have said, 'Mister, you have signed a contract!' He was an *absolute* man of honor."

Curry went on: "The next time I saw Lombardi was after the All-Star game six months later. Junior Coffey and I were the only All-Stars to report to Green Bay. Junior Coffey made the plane reservations on North Central Airlines. We had to be in Green Bay by midafternoon for practice. We got to the airport at the proper time, the Saturday morning after the game, but there was no record of our reservations. The North Central people said, 'We can get you as far as Milwaukee, for sure, but we're not sure you can get on beyond that because the flight from Milwaukee to Green Bay is completely booked.' So we got to Milwaukee and they came down the aisle of the plane to Green Bay and said, 'One of you has to get off.' Now, here's a Southern white boy sitting with Junior Coffey, who's a black guy from the University of Washington, both on our way to our first day with the Green Bay Packers and Vince Lombardi, and we're looking at each other to see which one's going to be late! Junior developed an upset stomach. A quick one. 'Aw, I'm sick,' he said.

"So I got off the plane in a fit of martyrdom and rage, so intimidated by the thought of being late that I mustered up my courage—quite unlike me—and I marched up to the North Central counter and announced that I wanted to see the president of the airline. They chuckled and said the president wasn't there. I started making a lot of noise. I said, 'Well, whoever the highest person in the airline is who's here, I want him out here!'

So they went and got some impressive-looking guy. I said, 'Sir, I am reporting to the Green Bay Packers today.'

"His eyes widened. At this time the Packers were just about the state religion in Wisconsin. When children were born, they were christened after the Packer backs. I said, 'I am going to work for a man named Lombardi, and I'm supposed to be there by three o'clock this afternoon, and North Central Airlines has bumped me off my airplane.'

"He said, 'Well, what would you like me to do about it?'

" 'All I know,' I said, "is that when I get there I'm going to tell Mr. Lombardi what happened, and from that little name-plate on your blazer, I know your name. He's going to know it, too.'

"He chartered . . . he *chartered* a Piper Cub and flew me to Manitowoc, Wisconsin, where there was a flight that got in to Green Bay by about two-thirty, and I was in St. Norbert College on time. Lombardi was waiting. I walked in and he said, 'Are you ready to go to work?'

"I said, 'Yes, sir.' "

"You didn't tell him what you'd gone through to get there?" I asked.

"Oh, heavens, no," Curry said. "Never, never. Never told him. Never came up in conversation somehow. One didn't bring up *any*thing except, 'Yes, sir.' 'No, sir.' "

Chapter 2

As we drove north from Louisville, Lombardi's name began to crop up increasingly—not surprising, since Curry had gone through a near-traumatic relationship with him (which was probably true of any Green Bay Packer), and the more I heard about him, the harder I pressed for details. I spent quite a lot of time saying, "What?" or "That's hard to believe," or most often, "Well, I don't see how you went on with someone like that."

Curry was patient. "You see, the key to him was that he believed that games are won not by systems, or superstar players, but by execution. So a player had to suffer the consequences of being driven to execute. Everything was directed at that. It was brilliantly simple. In fact, the technical part of football was much simpler than I thought it was going to be—the simplest of all the systems I played under. When I first got to Green Bay, Ken Bowman, who was the other center, went through all the plays with me in one afternoon. Then the next day, Lombardi himself sat down with me and on one sheet of a yellow legal pad he drew up every single play that the Green Bay Packers had. I think of all the documents, the awards, all the memorabilia of my career, and I'd give them up for that one sheet of paper, which I lost, or never thought was worth keeping. The famous one on the paper, of course, was the power sweep. Lombardi's theory was that nobody could stop the power sweep without giving away something else. So if they could stop 49, then you ran 37, which was an off-tackle play, because in order to stop the sweep they had to move the linebacker out. So then you ran inside him. There was no need for any fancy deception or anything of the sort, in his way of thinking. We had a reverse in our playbook. I don't think we ever ran it while I was there.

"So Lombardi's main theory was, 'You don't win games with systems; you win games with execution. Whatever the system is, you do it the same way every time.' So we would run the Green Bay power sweep five, ten, fifteen, twenty times in a row. The same play over and over. In the huddle the call for it was simply 49 or 48, depending on which direction we were going to run it. It was the play that made Jerry Kramer and Fuzzy Thurston famous, because they were the pulling guards and they'd come out around, leading Paul Hornung or Jimmy Taylor. If Jimmy was carrying the ball, it was called 38 or 39.

"Given this theory, everything depended on how you could execute. If you couldn't fit into the way he thought you should execute, well, then, that was the end of you there."

"How did he let his men go?" I asked. I had always been appalled by the methods of dismissing players in the NFL.

"If people went—were cut," Curry said, "there was no explanation. None needed. Lombardi never said, 'Well, we had to cut Joe Smith and John Black today.' They were just gone. The locker next door would be empty—like the guy had disappeared into thin air. Pat Peppler did the cutting for him. He was a big, bald, jovial guy, always with a grin on his face, who could do the painful job and I'm sure make it as painless as anybody.

He'd look in after breakfast and he'd say, 'The Coach wants to see you, and bring your playbook . . .' which meant, 'So long, Charlie.' On the day of the last cut my rookie year, I was sitting alone in my room. My roommate had been injured; he was in the hospital. I hadn't made the team for sure—there were some other good centers in camp—and I was sitting by myself, just apoplectic . . . waiting. Sure enough, there was a rap at the door. My heart jumped. I opened the door and it was Peppler. I could feel the blood just drain from my face.

"He said, 'Bill, my wife, Lindy, wants Carolyn to go to a luncheon with her tomorrow. Have Carolyn call her, would you?' and he turned and started to walk off.

"I leaned out the door. I said, 'Mr. Peppler, if you ever do anything like this to me again, I'm going to break your neck!' He turned around, bewildered. He didn't realize what he'd done. We laugh about it today. He scared me to death. I could've killed him.

"With that there was a huge letdown. I'd made the Packers . . . what I had aimed for all those years. I was a professional athlete. I had made the team, one of the best teams in the business. Then my good friend Rich Koeper, who had been the other rookie center and who had been moved from center to offensive tackle when I showed up from the All-Star game, came to my room and he said, 'Bill, could you help me load my stuff in the car?'

" 'What do you mean?'

" 'I'm leaving,' he said.

"He saw how low I looked. 'Hell, man,' he said, 'you've won the battle; you've defeated someone else. You've taken the job, and *you're* there instead of them.'

"But I felt none of that. I helped him load his things, and then I began to drive him to the motel where he was going to catch a limousine for the airport. I began to *weep.* I cried and cried and I couldn't stop! It was just humiliating . . . finally a big hero, stud athlete, and here I was making an ass of myself. Rich

10

Koeper was crying, too. That was a real scene."

"I'll say," I remarked.

He looked across at me from the wheel. "This is the second time in the last ten minutes that I've described myself weeping. . . . Well, that's a fair assessment of the sort of turmoil one felt being up there with the Packers."

By this time we were miles up Route 65, long past the great curve of the expressway above the candy-making factories in the north section of Louisville . . . out in the country with the heat beginning to build up, the air waves beginning to shimmer over the fields.

I asked Curry if there was a way one could distinguish a Green Bay Packer other than their habit of breaking down and weeping occasionally.

Curry grinned and said that one of the earmarks of the Green Bay Packers was their tremendous physical condition . . . that driven by Lombardi, a player had to be in shape, in *great* shape, to survive. "Take Jimmy Taylor, the great fullback," Curry explained. "He was just about the best-conditioned athlete I've ever seen. He knew that I had a background of having worked a little with weights. Not much; I'm not a power guy at all. But Jimmy would get me to lift weights with him between the morning and the afternoon practices. It'd be ninety-nine degrees and like a furnace outside. My locker was next to his. He'd say, 'Come on.' I'd say, 'Well, gee, Mr. Taylor, we've got to go back out and practice this afternoon.' 'Well, we're going to do our bench presses, kid.' And we'd go and do bench presses.

"It was worth it. Lombardi would just *destroy* you physically if you weren't in shape. The calisthenics period before practice was incredible—not fifteen side-straddle hops, but a *hundred*. Then at the conclusion of these calisthenics, which were led by a coach, Lombardi would walk up to the front of the group with a sadistic grin on his face and he'd say, 'Okay, let's go.' It was time for the grass drill. We'd start running in place. He wanted you to pick up those knees to your chest, and when he said,

11

'Down,' you'd dive on the ground; he'd say, 'Up,' and you'd jump to your feet, running in place. He would make you do them until you literally could not get off the ground. I've seen our offensive captain, Bob Skoronski, pass out. Guys were vomiting on the field, other guys could not get up off the ground, and he'd go over and say, 'Get up! Get up!' and they couldn't. That kind of thing.

"We'd just keep going. One time we did seventy-eight of them, up and down, which is an *awful* lot. Ken Bowman and I used to count them to keep from going insane with the pain. Willie Wood was famous for not . . . he would just quit! Lombardi'd say, 'Stop the drill!' which thrilled us because we could puff a bit. 'Willie, you're going to do those right! Now get going, you're going to do it for everybody.' Willie still couldn't do them. He'd fall down on the ground and he'd push himself up on one knee and then fall over again. You had to be as good a football player as Willie to be able to get away with that sort of thing. Finally Lombardi'd say, 'Oh, God, that's okay, okay,' and then we'd go on.

"Then, at the end of the grass drills, when everybody was just literally staggering, Lombardi would blow the whistle and we'd sprint around the goal post and back to the far end of the field . . . probably 250 yards, and you had to *sprint*. If you were last you were in big trouble. When you'd start to run after those grass drills, your legs wouldn't work! Literally would not function! They'd just wobble, and it took a conscious effort to get one in front of the other. Then you'd recover a bit and you'd get to where you were actually running and you'd get around to the far end of the field, when you'd get about thirty seconds to get a breath of air; everybody'd just drop to a knee and just gasp and pant . . . even losing an occasional breakfast and that sort of thing.

"I always took great pride in being in good shape and doing every grass drill. Some guys would watch Lombardi when he'd walk by them, and when he had his back to them they'd quit.

When he'd come back, then they'd get going again. Well, I always did every single one of them, and when he blew his whistle for the sprint I ran just as fast as I could. I wasn't fast enough to be first in from running around the goal post, but I always would *try* to be near.

"One day in my second year with the Packers, Jimmy Taylor came up to me and said, 'Now, Bill, you know you're a veteran now.' 'Yeah, that's right,' I said. 'You know you've gotta help set a good example for these young guys, these rookies.'

" 'Right.'

" 'Now, you know when we do our grass drills and run around the goal post?'

"I thought he was about to compliment me on how hard I tried.

" 'Well, when you get back over to the far end of the field . . . when we get to our little break, you know? Don't breathe so hard.'

" 'What?' I said. 'What do you mean, don't breathe so hard? I'm dying!'

" 'Well, you're in good shape,' he said, 'but you shouldn't be breathing so hard. These new guys, these rookies, will think you're tired and that you're not tough. Gotta be a tough guy.'

"I thought he was kidding. I started to laugh.

" 'I mean it,' he said. 'When you get back, blow it out. Then you'll feel all right. You don't have to be huffing and puffing.'

"Well, I thought: This man's crazy! The next morning I watched him. He did every single grass drill. He hit the ground, he picked his knees up higher than anybody else. In fact, Lombardi'd watch him and go crazy: 'Attaboy, Jimmy, attaboy! Look here, everybody, here's somebody in shape. Jimmy Taylor's always in shape!' That kind of thing. And he'd sprint around the goal post and come back. Sure enough! Everybody's dying and Jimmy Taylor was not breathing hard! He was just superbly conditioned. I thought I was in shape and I was just nothing compared to him. And then to match his physical heft he had

13

this supreme self-confidence. At meetings, during the film critiques, Lombardi would jump on him, and he'd just sit in the back of the room with his cigar and grin. He'd take a couple of puffs on that big cigar.

I interrupted. "Do you mean with all that emphasis on conditioning he'd let people smoke?"

"Yeah," Curry said. "You could even smoke in the locker room. This was one of the great shocks to me . . . when I'd come in and Hornung would light up at half-time. . . . Well, Lombardi'd jump on Jimmy for making a mistake that showed up in the films, and Jimmy would take a drag off his cigar, a big puff of smoke would drift up, and he'd look around and grin and flick the ash off the cigar like Groucho Marx and he'd say, 'Guess I'm washed up, Coach.' Unbelievable self-confidence.

"In practice he'd sneak off to the field where the kickers were. Lombardi'd yell at him, 'Taylor, get over heah—what you been up to?' and Taylor'd raise his arms up over his face defensively and he'd say, 'Coach, I was working on my field goal block.' He could get away with it because he was such an extraordinary football player. But then, of course, Taylor played out his option and went to play in New Orleans. It destroyed their relationship."

"I remember that," I said. "They never spoke again, did they?"

"Loyalty was such a big thing," Curry said. "Jimmy was a very tough negotiator on contracts, but Lombardi was too. Sometimes he would just tell a guy, 'You get your ass up there and sign that contract.' And they'd do it. Because of this one-on-one relationship with players, Lombardi hated agents. He told the guys, 'Don't send some agent in here to negotiate for you.' This was a long time before the lawyer-agent kind of representative got to be the vogue. Well, Jim Ringo thought he could take the chance. He was a great center for the Packers, and he probably regarded himself as almost indispensable because he called all the blocking—a key figure in the offensive line—and besides, he had this phenomenal reputation around the league. So he sent a lawyer, an agent, in to Lombardi's office to negotiate for him. The gentleman walked in and said, 'Mr. Lombardi, I'm here to represent Jim Ringo in his contract negotiations.' Lombardi said, 'You'll excuse me for a moment,' and he got up and left the room. About five minutes later he came back and he said, 'I'm sorry, you're talking to the wrong person.'

" 'I don't understand,' the agent said.

" 'Well, Jim Ringo now plays with the Philadelphia Eagles,' Lombardi said. 'You'll have to talk to them.' "

"And that's what happened with Taylor?" I asked.

"Something like that," Curry said. "Lombardi could not intimidate Jimmy into signing. He played out his option and went to play for New Orleans. I'm told Lombardi never forgave him. He never referred to him again by name. He called him 'the other guy.' They put Paul Hornung's jersey up in the Packer museum showcase, but not Taylor's. Lombardi said, 'We miss Hornung around here, but we could always do without the other guy.' "

I shook my head and remarked that I didn't understand how all that effort Taylor had made in his behalf—all those years of painful effort tearing through the middle of opposing lines—would not balance out just about *anything* that Lombardi could have held against him.

"He just wasn't an easy man," Curry said simply. "At times I couldn't stand the sight of him. Neither could the rest of us. I remember Gale Gillingham, his first week at Green Bay, was sitting in the back seat while somebody was driving us from practice back to the locker room. Gillingham had never said a word. In fact, I don't think I had heard him say a word since he'd arrived. He'd broken his right hand in the All-Star game, and he had a big cast on it. We'd had those awful grass drills. Of course, to Lombardi, there was no such thing as an injury. Gilly did every one of those grass drills with one hand. Everybody noticed him and realized: We've got one here; he's going to be all right! The rest of us were struggling to do them with *two*. Well, on the drive back, somebody said, 'Lombardi was *so* bad today.' You know the term that's applied when somebody's in an especially bad mood? 'He was on the rag today.' That was usually the comment somebody would make about him on an especially tough day. Well, Gillingham was sitting in the back seat and he suddenly said, unsolicited, the first words any of us had ever heard him say: 'That is the most disgusting man I've ever seen in my life.' I said, 'Boy, that sums it up.' "

"I would have sulked," I said. "I would have hang-dogged around just to show him how awful I thought he was."

Curry laughed. "There was no way you could manipulate him. And yet the devastating thing about *him*—which caused the love-hate relationship the players had with him—was the way he used his ability to manipulate *you*, to make you do whatever he wanted you to do. He could ruin your whole day in a matter of seconds. In the morning I'd be starting on my weight program and he'd walk in and scowl. I'd try to speak to him. He'd ignore me, or mumble something, and I hated him even more, and he'd get me thinking: What the hell am I *doing* in this business? And then ten minutes later he'd walk up and put his arm on my shoulder and say, 'I like the way you work. You're doing a good job, and I'm proud of you,' and I'd *die* for him! Do anything for him! Then the realization would come: My God, I'm being manipulated like a piece of Silly Putty. He flattens me out when he wants me flat. He makes me round and bounces me when he wants to bounce me. He *makes* me. . . . It was somehow demeaning, and yet at the same time it was exhilarating to be a part of all this because you knew—and I don't care what anybody says about him—that you were in the presence of greatness. Anybody who can move men like that.

"He completely dominated me for two football seasons, and to this day anytime I'm in a bind with a difficult problem to overcome, without exception I always think of him. Always! I think of him telling me, 'Son, the only thing you can do is to get off your ass and stop feeling sorry for yourself and overcome the pain and *do it.* Work out your method. Work out your system, and execute it. And don't tell me about a sprained ankle, and don't tell me that somebody's not being fair to you. I don't want to hear *any* of that. Do it!' That *always* rings in my mind."

"Well, was he fair?" I asked. "I mean in the sense of being equitable."

"Not especially," Curry said. "I remember one day in 1966 we were watching a film of a great game we had played the previous Sunday against the Cleveland Browns. It was the year after they had won the title. They just ate us up in the first half. The score was 14 to nothing when we went into the locker room. . . . Frank Ryan, their quarterback, was having a big day. We came out in the second half and began to peck away. Finally, with about two minutes left, the score was 20 to 14 in favor of the Browns. Lou Groza had kicked this mammoth forty-nine-yard field goal, which had hit the crossbar and bounced over for three points for them. With a couple of minutes left and six points behind, we started from our own twenty and gradually moved down the field. Finally, on their nine-yard line, it was fourth and goal, and time for a last play. Bart called a pass play. The wide receivers were covered, so he dumped it off to Jimmy Taylor in the flat. There were three tacklers—you've got to see this to believe it—and all they had to do was get him on the ground and the game was over. Well, he went by the first, around the second, and he ran over a third, and got into the end zone. We kicked the extra point and won the game 21 to 20. You can imagine the satisfaction. It was very hot. When I weighed in after the game I weighed 218 pounds. I had lost fourteen pounds.

"But in the film Lombardi began to notice *my* afternoon. I had been playing against Vince Costello, who was a very good middle linebacker. He was a very cagey guy. The week before, Lombardi had told me the way to work on him when we ran our sweep was not to take a sharp angle to cut him off, because

17

he'd get around behind me to make the play. He wanted me to take an angle more directly at him, which is an unusual way to do it. Well, I did what the coach said. Costello beat me all day long. It was painfully obvious in the film that Tuesday. I'd go flying straight at him. He just ignored me. I'd miss him completely, and he'd make the tackle on Hornung or somebody. Lombardi stopped the projector and ran it back again. He didn't say a word. Ran it back again. Ran it back once more. Finally he stopped the projector, and in the dark I could see those glasses turn toward me. He said, 'Curry, you know that's God-awful.' All my teammates were sitting there. He said, 'How would you describe that?' Well, I was just burning. I was just *dying* to say, 'Coach, you *told* me to do it that way!' But of course I didn't. He went on, 'We're going to look at this again.' He ran it again, and then he went into one of his tirades. 'That's God-awful! You stink! *You* stink! And you know something else? Your snaps for punts have been stinking, too.' It went on for five minutes or so."

"I don't understand why you didn't get up and tell him, 'Well, you told me to, Coach.' " I said.

"Because," Curry replied, "all this time it kept running through my mind that though I kept excusing myself because, really, he *had* told me to use that technique, the point was that the only thing that matters is: Did you accomplish your mission? And if you didn't, there's no such thing as an excuse."

"Did anyone stand up to him?" I asked.

"Just about the only person who could handle these critiques was Fuzzy Thurston. Fuzzy would sit up in front, and when he knew that one of his bad plays was coming up, he'd begin to rant and rave before Lombardi could. It was really a riot. Some behemoth would thrash by Fuzzy, who'd missed his block— someone like Roger Brown of the Detroit Lions, who weighed three hundred pounds, and even before Roger could get into the backfield and crush Bart to the ground, Fuzzy'd be saying, 'Oh, look at that! Isn't that the worst block you've ever seen!

That's awful!' Lombardi, in spite of himself, would have to laugh. He'd say, 'Fuzzy, you're right. That's *bad*. Okay, next play.' And Fuzzy could get away with it!

"Really no one was immune. The great veterans . . . everybody—it didn't make any difference. I remember him saying things to Jerry Kramer, who was an All-Pro guard. 'Did you see that, Jerry? Do you think that you're worth what we're paying you? Do you think for a minute that your football deserves the kind of dollars that you're getting?'

"Jerry'd be sitting there, a huge, powerful guy, literally leaning backward and bending the back of his metal folding chair in anguish. Just a devastating kind of thing! You asked about Lombardi being fair. Henry Jordan's great contribution about playing under Lombardi was: 'Lombardi is very fair: he treats us all alike—like dogs.'

"As he moved around the practice field, it was a presence that you could sense. It motivated people to perform. It wasn't malevolent. It scared. It was unique. Joe Thomas, when he was general manager of the Colts, had a presence when he appeared on the field . . . but it was sort of debilitating; everybody got tense and angry when he came around. When Lombardi came around, everybody got afraid . . . but highly active. The voice, like the personality, had just the most indescribable intensity. Everything he said was for effect. One day while we were practicing, a little dog came out and started prancing around the practice field. Nobody could concentrate because he was running in and out between people's legs. Just a cute little setter dog. Guys were trying to shoo him away—'Go! Go!'—and he'd scamper off and then run back, wagging his tail and having a good time. Lombardi was about sixty yards away at the other end of the field and suddenly this voice came booming from down there: *'Get the hell off the field!'* I swear I saw this happen: the dog tucked his tail between his legs, and the last time we saw him he was rounding a corner two blocks away from the field."

We drove on for a while through the Indiana countryside; The green overhang sign announced that we were coming up on a state road that swung off to a town called Franklin. We started chatting about other matters. Curry began talking about stereo equipment, but abstractedly, his mind still on Lombardi, and suddenly he said, "The difficult thing to articulate is how really forceful his presence was. Jerry Kramer didn't get it in his book, *Instant Replay*. He just didn't capture it. Nobody has. They did a TV show with Ernest Borgnine and it was just pathetic. Borgnine wasn't pathetic—Borgnine was superb. But they decided the Lombardi story was about a man going from New York, where he'd hoped to be a head coach, to an obscure town in Wisconsin that his wife didn't like. Crazy. The real story should have been about this man's ability to shock, to frighten, to overpower other people with whatever means he had to use. On the first day he gathered the team together, he always showed the film of the championship game from the year before. He didn't comment on it; he just showed it, whether the Packers were in it or not. And then he'd turn off the projector and he'd say, 'Gentlemen, I have no illusions about what's going to happen to me if I don't win. So don't you have any illusions about what's going to happen to you if you don't produce for me. . . . There are three things that're important in your life: your religion, your family, and the Green Bay Packers—in that order.' And then, as soon as we'd get on the field, he'd get the order mixed up in his own mind. What was paramount was— by whatever means—to build in you that sense that you had to be the best ever. When I first came to pro ball I just wanted to make the team; then when I did I decided I sure would like to be first-string; then after that I made All-Pro, and I thought: Now I want to be All-Pro every year. The obsession to be best was precisely Lombardi's. Time and time again he'd say things like this: 'When you go on the field, I want you thinking about one thing—that is, For this day I'm going to be the greatest center in football. When those people walk out of the stands, I want that guy to turn to his wife and say, "We just saw the greatest offensive center who ever played." '

"So he had this uncanny talent for manipulating people to be exactly what he wanted them to be. He would select a role for each player. He wrote the play, he did the choreography, and if you didn't fit the role, he would change your personality so that you could play the part. If you didn't like the role, it didn't make any difference; he manipulated you and made you what he wanted you to be until you could play it better than anybody else in the National Football League. *Or* he would get rid of you. I heard him tell Steve Wright, who was a guy who grinned a lot—he'd miss a block and come back to the huddle with a smile on his face, which would drive Lombardi insane—'Goddammit, Wright, you think that's funny! You're never gonna be a man! You're never gonna make it! *Yes,* you are! *I'm* gonna make you, I'm gonna create you. I'm gonna make you into something before I'm through with you.'

"I heard him tell another guy, 'I'm gonna make you work. I'm gonna make you hurt before I get rid of you!' And he did get rid of him. That was Rich Marshall. He had this forefinger cut off at the knuckle so that when he took his stance it looked like he'd stuck a finger in the ground. He got a lot of kidding about it. 'Git your finger out of the ground, Marshall!' "

"How Lombardi treated him just seems arbitrarily cruel," I commented. "What do you truly think he thought of all you players?"

Curry thought for a while, and then he said, "This will be argued by some players, but I believe that Lombardi really did love us. I don't think he could've appealed to our better instincts if we didn't feel that he really cared about us. I've seen him cry when we lost a game. Here we go again—those weeping Packers. It wasn't for appearance' sake. I mean, I've just seen the tears in his eyes. Of course, it was foremost because *he* had lost. But he also had genuine affection for . . . he liked to be around 'the guys.' He wanted to be accepted. When he was admonishing us about our behavior, he used to say things to us like: 'Don't you think that I'd like to go get drunk downtown, too? Don't you think I'd like to go out and do that? Don't you think I'd like you guys to like me? I know you don't like me. But I don't give a crap about that. We're here to do a job. Your liking me is not near as important as winning football games. So I don't *care* if you like me.' That kind of thing. Every now and then it would surface, but it was very rare. He was such an odd contradiction. He was very profane, yet he went to church every day; he was a daily celebrant, Catholic, very devout. He considered the priesthood at one point. Bart Starr said, 'When I heard about this man taking over the team in 1959, I could hardly wait to meet a man that went to church every day.' Then he went on to say, 'I worked for him for two weeks and then I realized this man *needs* to go to church every day.' "

Curry shifted slightly in his seat behind the steering wheel. "You were asking me a while back if anyone stood up to him. I remember Starr one time. We were in Cleveland playing an exhibition game. Lombardi was into one of his tirades up and down the sidelines. Our offense was driving—Bowman was the center—and they got to Cleveland's four-yard line with a first down when Bart took too long in the huddle and they marched off a delay-of-game penalty against him. Lombardi went insane. He started *screaming:* 'What the hell's going on out there?' This terrible voice that everyone in that huge stadium—there were 81,000 people there—could hear. I saw Bart slip back out of the huddle to glare at Lombardi; then he called the play and threw a touchdown pass to Boyd Dowler.

"At this point I started out on the field, trotting past Lombardi, to snap the ball for the extra point. That was my job. But to my surprise I saw Starr coming toward us—which was odd because he was supposed to be the holder for the extra-point play. So I stopped . . . baffled. I thought perhaps he was hurt. As he got alongside me, about fifteen feet from Lombardi, he yelled out at the top of his lungs and just *laced* him with the most incredible verbal barrage."

"I almost went to my knees. Bart Starr! This kind and decent churchman, one of the gentlest people, never a word of profanity or anything of the sort, and here he was yelling these things at Lombardi in a big, booming, resonant voice. I turned around and Lombardi was standing there, just agape; he couldn't believe it either. Well, we ran on the field, kicked the extra point, and nothing was said about it. Lombardi didn't say another word the rest of that game—truly stunned probably—and he was nice to us for about two weeks after that. Then he began to get mean again.

"We had a sort of war council, in which there were about six guys—Bob Skoronski, who was the offensive captain, and Tom Moore and Bart and Paul Hornung, guys like that—and every now and then when things got really bad, about once a year, they'd go to Lombardi and say, 'Coach, you're going to have to let up. You're driving us all crazy! We can't function under this withering kind of abuse.' Maybe he'd let up for a day or two. Maybe we'd have a good game, and he'd be nice for a few days. But then we'd have a bad game, and he'd stomp back in on Tuesday morning and everybody'd just be sitting there aquiver. He'd say, 'I tried it your way. I'm sick and tired of being father confessor for a bunch of yellow, no-good punks. The whip! That's the only thing you understand. And I'm going to whip you again, and drive you, make you! Why do I always have to make you? Don't you think I get tired of being this way?' Once again everybody would squirm and feel that somehow they'd made the wrong choice for a profession: What am I doing with this person here? Why? But invariably he would come back in the next breath and win everybody over again . . . although sometimes you couldn't imagine how he could do it.

"Once in 1965 we had been to Los Angeles and had lost a game to the Rams that we *had* to win. Los Angeles was the last-place team in the league and they just *stomped* us. On the way back Lionel Aldridge—the big defensive end—began to sing. A couple of beers and he was singing! Lombardi heard about it. Well, on Tuesday morning he came into the meeting and he began to question Lionel's ancestry. He got into such an emotional shouting binge that it was like one of those tirades you'd see in films of Hitler going through a frenzy—though I don't mean to draw any parallel. I'm talking about awesome, forceful personalities, not the quality of what they did or the kind of people they were. Finally Lombardi said, 'I want all the assistant coaches out of this room and all the doors shut. I want to be here with these football players . . . if that's what you can call them.' So everybody cleared out. Scurried out."

"The assistant coaches?" I asked.

"Oh, yes. The assistant coaches were terrified of him, too. Absolutely. You could hear him in the next room dressing *them* down the same way he did us, though of course he never did it in front of us.

"When the coaches were out and the doors were shut, Lombardi really went at it. The meeting seemed to go on for an hour and a half, with Lombardi screaming, shouting: 'Goddammit, you guys don't care if you win or lose. I'm the only one that cares. I'm the only one that puts his blood and his guts and his heart into the game! You guys show up, you listen a little bit, you concentrate . . . you've got the concentration of three-year-olds. You're nothing! I'm the only guy that gives a damn if we win or lose.'

"Suddenly there was a stirring in the back of the room, a rustle of chairs. I turned around and there was Forrest Gregg, on his feet, bright red, with a player on either side, holding him back by each arm, and he was straining forward. Gregg was another real gentlemanly kind of guy, very quiet. Great football player. Lombardi looked at him and stopped. Forrest said, 'Goddammit, Coach . . . excuse me for the profanity.' Even at his moment of rage, he was still both respectful enough and intimidated enough that he stopped and apologized. Then he went on: ' 'Scuse the language, Coach, but it makes me sick to hear you say something like that. We lay it on the line for you every Sunday. We live and die the same way you do, and it hurts.' Then he began straining forward again, trying to get up there to punch Lombardi out. Players were holding him back. Then Bob Skoronski stood up, very articulate. He was the captain of the team. 'That's right,' he said. 'Dammit, don't you tell us that we don't care about winning. That makes me sick. Makes me want to puke. We care about it every bit as much as you do. It's our knees and our bodies out there that we're throwing around.'

"So there it was. The coach had been confronted, the captain of a ship facing a mutinous crew, with the first mate standing and staring him down face to face, and it truly looked as though he had lost control of the situation.

"But then damned if the master didn't triumph again. After just a moment's hesitation, he said, 'All right. Now, *that's* the kind of attitude I want to see. Who else feels that way?'

"Well, at this very moment, Willie Davis was nervously rocking back and forth on his metal folding chair. Willie was known as Dr. Feelgood on the team because every day at practice, with everybody limping around and tired and moaning and complaining, somebody always looked over and asked, 'Willie, how you feel?' He always said the same thing: 'Feel *good,* man!' So there was Dr. Feelgood rocking back and forth and you know how those chairs are. He lost his balance and he fell forward! He fell right out into the middle of the room . . . onto his feet; it looked as if he had leapt from his chair just as Lombardi asked, 'Who else feels that way?' And Willie sort of grinned sheepishly and he said, 'Yeah, me, too! I feel that way, man!' Lombardi said, 'All right, Willie, that's great.' And it swept through the room; everybody said, 'Yeah, hell—me, too!' and suddenly you had forty guys that could lick the world. That's what Lombardi created out of that situation. He went around to each player in that room with the exception of the rookies—he skipped the four of us rookies—and as he looked in each man's face he said,

'Do you want to win football games for me?' And the answer was, 'Yes, sir,' forty times. He wended his way through that mass of people sitting around in that disarray of chairs and looked each guy nose to nose two inches from his face and he said that thing: 'Do you want to win football games?' and every man said, 'Yes, sir,' and we did not lose another game that year."

Chapter 3

Not far beyond the Franklin turnoff we stopped and took a walk to stretch a bit. Curry trotted ahead of me across the field and I could see he was thinking about the hamstring. We walked nearly out of earshot of the traffic humming by on the distant expressway and sat down in the shade of a tree. It was hot, but the ground was cool, and I thought back on the quick pleasure of flopping down in the shade when the breaks came in the training-camp practices.

Curry was wearing one of his championship rings—he was entitled to three of them, including two Super Bowls—enormous, cumbersome things that always struck me as looking like part of a brass knuckle. I remarked on it and Curry said he was wearing the first ring he'd won—his rookie year with Lombardi. He took it off and passed it over. The design showed a representation of the Packer stadium, Lambeau Field, with a diamond sitting on top.

"I've had all my rings appraised," Curry said as I passed it back to him, "and this, of the three championship rings I have, is the least expensive. I happen to think it's kind of special, because it was my first year. To have this ring is still a special thing to me. When I get depressed, sometimes I can actually *feel* it there, and it makes me think of Lombardi. I wear it most all the time. The Colts Super Bowl ring I wear on occasion; that meant a lot to me, as you know, because we accomplished a lot without too much ability on that team . . . and because of Coach Don McCafferty. I wore it in Los Angeles last year because Carroll Rosenbloom was there."

"I'm surprised they can't think of something else to give," I commented. "I mean, after one ring it's not all that interesting to get another. The wives must fret. They'd like a new wing on the house or something."

"Well, Lombardi always gave something to the wives, too," Curry said. "In 1965 he gave them—guess what?—beautiful dinner rings. Some of the wives didn't like them. They were white gold, tourmaline with an oblong shape, like a football, with a diamond in the middle. Very pretty, I thought. But in 1962, I think it was, Lombardi had given the wives fur stoles. Apparently almost all of them sent him a thank-you note. Well, in '65 when he gave those rings, very few of them sent thank-you notes. The rings didn't match up to those stoles. I guess he was pretty upset about it. In Chicago at the beginning of my second year, I took Carolyn to a get-together of the team after the college All-Star game. She's an easy person to know after a while, but she can be painfully shy with somebody like Lombardi, or some authority figure out of her element. She was reticent, but she wanted to thank him face to face and make up for not having written a note. So she walked up and said, 'Coach Lombardi, I love this ring. I wasn't sure . . .' She sort of stumbled. She said, 'I just wasn't quite sure who to thank.'

" 'Young lady,' he said, 'there is only one person that you could possibly thank.'

"With that she almost passed out. She said, 'Oh, well, then, thank you very much, Coach.' I think that's the last time that she ever talked to him. He didn't mean anything by it. But he was just so blunt and direct. He made me mad at the time because she was trying to be nice."

"Bill, what went on if something nice happened?" I asked. "Like a winning streak, or a great victory?"

"Well, he'd rejoice, of course," Curry said, "but he'd always let us know that it was a one-man show. If we got on a winning streak, he'd say things to us like: 'Don't think you're responsible for all this success. . . . Don't let it go to your heads and become impressed with yourselves, because I want you to understand that *I* did this. *I* made you guys what you are.' We'd all stare at him. We loathed him. Then he'd be back at it. He'd say, 'I'm going to drive you, and whip you, and embarrass you, and humiliate you. I'm going to kick you in the butt if I have to, physically. . . . I'm going to do whatever I have to do to make you *go.*' And then he'd say, 'If I think you don't hate the Rams' —the week we were playing the Rams—'on Thursday, let me promise you that by Sunday you'll hate *me* so much that you'll go out and destroy somebody.' "

"That was a tactic of his?" I asked.

"Sure. He had this thing that you had to hate your opponent. He said, 'You respect him, but you hate him. He's trying to take your livelihood away from you. You *have* to hate him. There's no way around that!'

"That's not you at all," I said.

"No; this was where he and I had a big parting of the ways: I never felt that was necessary. Of course, I never argued with him about it. We just listened. We'd hear that sort of thing at team meetings . . . in a kind of philosophizing period where he'd come up with his sayings and quotes and what he wanted us to remember that day. Let's see if I can remember a couple." Bill peered up through the branches of the tree. 'Fatigue makes cowards of us all.' 'Perfect physical conditioning is absolutely essential to victory.' 'The harder a man works, the harder it is

29

for him to surrender.' A lot of military sayings. In fact, when I saw the movie *Patton,* I was stunned at the similarity between the two characters. There's that great scene where George C. Scott, playing the general, discovers his unit and it's battered to pieces and the young lieutenant or captain or whoever is sitting propped up against a devastated tank. Patton asks him how it went. The officer says, 'Well, sir, it ended up hand-to-hand, and most of the troops are gone. It was bad.' Patton leans over and kisses the guy on the forehead. Then he walks out across the battlefield and he gazes at all the ruin and the loss of life and the insanity of it all, and he says, 'I love it, God help me, I do love it so.' From my own personal standpoint, that is how I regard football, and I think Lombardi looked at it the same way. I know at one time he thought about the priesthood and then at another time he studied law; but he always came back to football. He was caught in it. He had to do it, and he had to do it better than anybody had ever done it. At one time he thought he could step aside—that it would probably have been better for his health because he was so animated and involved with the game. He resigned, but then after one year, probably after *ten minutes,* he saw that it just wasn't realistic to think that he could stay out of it. He *had* to go to coach the Washington Redskins."

I asked Curry if there was one element that seemed common to all coaches, Lombardi included. He said that the one common thread that he had seen run through the great coaches— or the great motivators in any walk of life—was that they were true to themselves, and that they did not make an effort to be something they weren't. Don McCafferty, who coached at the Colts after Don Shula left, could never scream at anybody; so he never tried. And he produced winning teams.

"What about Shula?" I asked.

"Don Shula, of course, was not nearly as colorful as Lombardi. The guys on the Colts would come in after practice and say, 'If he screams like that at us again, I don't know what I'm going to do.' I just laughed. I said, 'That's not screaming.' Compared to Lombardi, Shula sounded like Mrs. Douglas Lyle, who was my Sunday school teacher at College Park Presbyterian. But Shula was very interested in how Lombardi had done things. He would occasionally meander over and ask, 'How did Lombardi handle that kind of situation?' I'd tell him what I thought. Of course, Shula didn't always do what Lombardi had done. He did it his own way. But he was very curious. He had the same intense kind of drive, but its force was not as evident as Lombardi's. If somebody asked me to describe in one phrase what Lombardi was, he was a force field. When he came in a room, everybody in that room had to respond. He aroused emotions in people to a greater extent than anybody I've ever known. Some people can yell at you and you chuckle because they're ridiculous, the way they do it. But when he did it, it would go straight to your heart and your heart would go straight to your throat. You just choked. He could make you cry—as by now you well know. He could elicit the damnedest, deepest reaction from you. He was a walking, living, breathing piece of motivation all the time; he never shut off, never turned off.

"This thing about winning . . . In Green Bay my second year, Ken Bowman was still the first-string center and we were playing Pittsburgh in an exhibition game. In the second quarter Bowman dislocated his shoulder badly. He was out. So I went in the game until, in the fourth quarter, somebody kicked me in the head. Gave me just a wacky feeling; I didn't know where I was or anything. I went back in the huddle and Bart called the play. We went up to the line of scrimmage and I got down in my stance. Bart called the signals: 'Set, 1, 48, hut, *hut.*' The count was on the second *hut,* at which ten people fired off the ball and went into their blocks. Bart came out from under the center and the backs began to run. I was still in my stance with the ball under my hand. The ball had never moved. So the whistles went and we were penalized. Everybody gathered around. 'What the hell is wrong with you! What are you doing?' I said, 'I don't know.' Forrest Gregg, or somebody, said, 'Oh-oh.

Somebody hit you in the head.' I said, 'I think so.' They asked, 'Are you all right now?' and I said, 'Yeah, I think I'm all right.'

"We went back in the huddle, and another play was called. The identical thing happened. So the coaches came out on the field and led me off to the sidelines; Bob Skoronski came in to finish up the game at center. In the locker room they helped me to get undressed. I was in a complete stupor; it's a euphoric kind of thing where everybody looks strange and you don't recognize anybody. It had happened to me in high school once, and I had gone into a fit of crying. I don't know what part of the brain is affected. This time it seemed funny to me and I was sitting there chuckling. To be sure that I got to my car and home all right, they let Carolyn come in to fetch me. It's the only time I know of a woman getting into an NFL locker room. She's still very proud that she got to come in there and see what everything looked like.

"So she came in and got me, and we walked out. I'll never forget the feeling of looking at the field and at the scoreboard of Lambeau Field, Green Bay, Wisconsin, and remarking to Carolyn that I had never been there before. I said, 'This is a strange place.' I remember her laughing. She could laugh because the doctors had assured her that I was all right, and besides, she had seen me go through this before. So we went over to the team function after the game, which was required, win or lose. Everybody had to go to the party and eat cold cuts and things.

"Lombardi called to me across the room: 'Curry! Curry! You all right?'

" 'Yessir.'

" 'Do you know where you are?'

" 'No, sir,' I said.

"I remember him shaking his head and chuckling. 'Do you know what we're doing?'

" 'No, sir.'

"But this is the poignant thing. He said, 'Who won the game?'

" 'We did,' I said.

"It was the only thing I remembered. We had won the game! It stuck in my mind. Where everything else had just completely left, that was there. And Lombardi wanted to be sure it was."

"Damn, that's a good story," I said.

We sat and watched the cloud patterns across the fields. Down on the expressway the big rigs went by and we could hear the distant whine of the tires.

"Was it easy leaving a coach like that?" I asked.

"I can remember every instant of it," Curry said. "On February 16, 1967, my phone rang at eight-thirty in the morning and woke me up. The voice said, 'Bill, this is Coach Lombardi.'

"I said, 'Yes, sir.'

" 'I've got some sad news for you,' he said. 'I had to put you on the expansion list, and the New Orleans Saints claimed you.'

"I was stunned. I was a starter. There was a lot of emotion in his voice. 'I'm just sorry,' he said. 'I don't know any better way to explain it to you than I have. I'm just sorry.'

After a second or so, I said, 'Well, Coach, I want you to know that these have been two of the finest years of my life with respect to learning what to expect of myself and how to extract that and how to do things that I didn't think I could do.' And he said, 'Well, you're a fine young man and we're going to miss you.' I said, 'Thank you,' and that was it."

"It doesn't sound as if it was too hard. You must have been relieved—" I began to say:

"Oh, no." Curry looked over. "You've got it wrong. It was traumatic. He hung up the phone and I just *completely* fell apart. Carolyn was sitting there. 'What is it? What is it? What is it?' and I just cried for probably an hour. It was a tremendous blow. It must have been a bad day for Lombardi, too. He had to put Paul Hornung, who was his favorite, on the list, too, and Paul was claimed. Paul had run out of gas; he'd been playing too long, but it must have been emotionally upsetting. Then the reaction began to set in. I became bitter. I had wanted to be a success under Vince Lombardi and I just hadn't been. It rankled and I held it against him. I remember before the Super Bowl game against the Jets, Bill Wallace of the *New York Times* spent some time with me, asking for a comparison between Don Shula and Lombardi. I said that I preferred Shula's methods: he was tough and hard but not abrasive, and he didn't annihilate a man's ego, or harass him. The headline in the sports page of the *Times* the next day read: LOMBARDI NOT CURRY'S DISH. Bill wrote pretty much what I said, but it came out sounding more acerbic and critical than I meant it to."

"Did you ever meet him again?" I asked.

"Strange thing," Curry said. "Paul Hornung and I had run into each other in New Orleans at the Super Bowl that year when the Kansas City Chiefs had beaten the Vikings, and the two of us had got into a big argument about what would happen if I ever *did* run into Lombardi. Paul had said, 'You shouldn't have said those things about the old man.' I didn't put much stock in that because I remembered the father-son relationship between the two of them. Paul said, 'You're just wrong. He doesn't dislike you, or any of the players.' I replied that if we happened to meet, he wouldn't have the time of day for me. Paul was scornful. 'If he ran into you right now, he'd say, "Bill, it's great to see you, how are you? I'm so glad to see that you're doing well." ' We got into a pretty stiff argument. It went on for a couple of hours in Jean Lafitte's Absinthe House on Bourbon Street.

"Well, it wasn't a month later that I ran into Lombardi at the President's Prayer Breakfast in Washington. Paul was absolutely right. Lombardi's reaction was almost verbatim the way Paul had said it would be. I felt ashamed, and I said at the time, 'I'd like to visit with you, Coach.' He said, 'Well, I'd like to see you, too, and visit.' It was all very sincere and the first time I'd really felt close to him at all. This would have been February of 1970, and only a few months later he was stricken with cancer. When that happened we were in the midst of negotiations in Washington with the owners. Bob Long was in town—he had played in Green Bay with me, and then later in Atlanta and Los Angeles, and finally with the Redskins under Lombardi. He came by the hotel one day and said, 'You know, Coach Lombardi's at Georgetown Hospital. Let's go see him.'

"I didn't know we would be able to get into his room, so I sat down and wrote a long letter about the way things had happened and how I had come to have such great regard for him. We walked into the hospital. Mrs. Lombardi was sitting just outside the elevator when we got off. Sonny Jurgensen, the Washington quarterback, was there with her, along with Coach Lombardi's brother. She went to see if he was resting, but it was okay and so we walked in. I was very nervous. Bob and I had gone by the cathedral, where a priest had said a mass for him, and we had little cards signed by the priest, which we took in.

"You're never really prepared for what cancer can do to somebody physically. This robust, powerful man, this great presence, who had been reduced physically to a . . . well, he wasn't in the final stages, but he had begun to wither physically. His right arm was full of needles and tubes, so I took his left hand, and his grip was still very firm. I remember the conversation precisely. I said, 'Coach, I didn't know if I was going to be able to see you, so I wrote in a letter the things I wanted to say.' I guess I was hoping that I would not have to say these things directly to him—not what I really felt—but then it all just tumbled out. I said, 'Coach, some of the things that you've read have been true and some of them are misprints; some of them were taken out of context. But I just want you to know that honestly, without bitterness, looking at the time I spent with you, you've really meant a lot to my life.' He gripped my hand. He looked me straight in the eye, and he said, 'Bill, you can mean a lot to my life right now if you can pray'—not the words of a desperate man, but those of a man with implicit faith. With that, I couldn't speak anymore. I just nodded.

"I walked out of the room with Mrs. Lombardi. It was all quite tense and I was very choked up. When we got out in the hall she said, 'Yeah, I didn't appreciate that stuff that you said in the paper at all!' I said, 'Well, Mrs. Lombardi'—she's the last person whose wrath I wanted to incur—'I've grown up a lot. I just didn't appreciate the boost or the kick in the butt at the time, and now I do!'

"Then she went into this litany, almost: 'Why is it? He's fifty-seven years old. He's too young; he's got too much to do! It's such a shame. How can it happen?!' I said, 'Well, I don't know, maybe it won't happen. These things have turned around before.' She said, 'You know what he did? He asked the doctor the other day what his odds were. The doctor replied, "Well, Coach, I have had eighty-four people with this type of cancer —cancer of the colon—and all of them have been terminal." He said, "I didn't ask you that. I asked you what *my* odds are." The doctor said something like, "Well, I suppose ten thousand to one." He said, *"I* will beat it." ' And he believed it! Even with this incredible stuff eating away at his body, he had the same force of will . . . and I'm convinced that to the moment he died, he didn't believe he was going to. It reminded me of what he used to say to us all the time, which I thought was absurd when he first started saying it: 'I have never lost a football game. Never! Now, a few times the clock runs out too early. But that doesn't mean we would've lost, because if we'd had one more minute or one more quarter . . . if we'd played long enough, we would've caught 'em and beat 'em.' He really believed that. That's the way he talked about his life. That had just an awesome impact on me as a person.

"The upshot of my experience with Lombardi is that I did not see for the longest time that what he was doing would end up having a positive effect on us, especially on me. I saw it as a negative thing . . . a repressive, frightening kind of presence. Whereas, in retrospect—and it's not a reaction of sympathy over his death, because I had determined this for myself before he ever came down with cancer—I realized that he had pushed me through a sort of barrier, a self-pity barrier. He taught me that I could do things with pain, transcend it. That's what he forced us to do . . . in a physical sense. There were awful examples of it. Bob Long had a bad knee; he got it hit in practice one day. He lay there on the ground and just writhed. It was caught on film—this player rolling over and grabbing his knee. Plain enough he was in terrible pain.

"Lombardi cut off the film. 'Long, if I ever—*ever*—see another performance like that out of you, and I do mean performance, you'll be out of there so fast it'll make your head swim.'

"Just awful. And yet Bob Long will tell you that Lombardi turned his life around, made him a successful person. Bob went on to Atlanta. He was in an incredible car accident in which he broke his back. He was left on the junk pile of the NFL. Lombardi came and redeemed him, and put him back to work on the Redskins—and Bob will never forget him for that, or for providing him with a sense of how to survive what he'd been through."

We sat there for a while, Curry turning the big ring on his finger. "Maybe you can see why I wear this one more than the others," he said. "Especially this trip." He stood up and stretched, and we headed back across the fields for the expressway.

Chapter 4

We had lunch in a pleasant enough inn a few miles off the expressway, in a dining room with a mural running the length of one wall depicting an early-American river scene, a vast panorama with a great many things going on—a stagecoach coming down to the water's edge and a ferry starting out across from the opposite bank, and some Indians standing under a grove of trees, "friendlies," we decided, because two of them were smoking pipes—such a busy landscape that my impression was it subdued the conversation in the room. People would sneak a look at it and get lost in contemplation, like crowds in front of a dioramic display in a museum.

We looked at it for a while, and then edged our chairs around so we could communicate better. I was curious about the difference between the two great teams Bill had played for—the Packers and then the Colts, to whom the Saints had traded him almost as soon as they got their hands on him from Green Bay.

"Well, the extraordinary thing," Curry said, "was how unimposing the Colts looked when I checked in at their training camp. The physical specimens on the Green Bay Packers had been unbelievable. Standing in the Packers locker room you had the strong impression that everyone there could push over a wall. But when I reported to the Colts we had a weigh-in day, standing around buck naked to step on the scales, and I looked at the bodies on the Colt team, and wondered if we'd ever win a game. It was like wandering into the locker room of the YMCA. . . . Tom Matte, a sort of chubby halfback, the famed John Unitas himself, who certainly wasn't much of a physical specimen, looking like a pair of pliers standing there. Unitas and Earl Morrall, the backup quarterback, were called 'Hump' and 'Rump'—Unitas for his slumped posture, and Earl because he was about two ax handles in girth across that area. Then we had Alex Hawkins, who was slow and crippled most of the time, and Don Shinnick, who was a linebacker, of all things, and yet he had probably the strangest body in the history of the world; Jimmy Orr was one of the top receivers there ever was, but he truly disliked body contact (if you can believe that of a football player) and on plays when he was supposed to block, he assumed a weird posture which we called a 'fire hydrant block,' a three-point stance like a poodle at a hydrant, which you can imagine was not especially formidable. Who else? Well, Glenn Ressler thought so little of his body that he never built it up with weights or ever took off his shirt to get himself a tan: he looked like the underside of something. And then Dan Sullivan, an offensive guard—square body with short legs, and—hell, you remember *you* beat him, or came awfully close, in the forty-yard dash."

"My God, you're right," I said.

"But he was an incredible football player," Curry went on, "even if he did look like an executive for Mrs. Filbert's margarine, which is exactly what he was in the off-season. Of course, my body isn't that much either. It's skinny and fat . . . thin legs, big butt. So maybe Lombardi figured I'd fit in better with these people. And yet these people—this odd amalgam of the lean and the fat—damned if they weren't the champions." Curry turned slightly. He was staring at the mural. "Where do you suppose that river is? Do you suppose it's real?"

"I can't imagine," I said truthfully. "Look at those strange humped blue hills."

We stared at the mural while the meal was set before us. The waitress did not know. She had been told once, because sometimes people asked, but she had forgotten. "The Ohio?" she said tentatively. She began taking an order at the next table.

"Who was Alex Hawkins?" I asked, to bring Curry around.

"A very pertinent question," Curry said. "People talk about linemen being monuments to anonymity . . . but think of the people on the special teams. Shula tried to give Hawkins recognition by naming him the first special teams' captain in the NFL —captain of the kickoff team and so forth. That gave him the privilege of walking out for the pregame coin toss. When he walked out for the first time with the other captains—I think Marchetti was the defensive captain at the time and Unitas was the offensive captain, two such towering names—the referee said to the opposing captains, 'This is Captain Marchetti, Captain Unitas, and Captain Hawkins.' One of the other captains said, 'Captain *who?*' So he's been known as Captain Who for about the last ten years.

"Old Captain Who! Every week he had an award for the outstanding performer on the special teams. He would leave the stadium after a game on Sunday—nice suit on, nice tie, all spiffed up. Our next practice was Tuesday morning at nine o'clock; everybody'd be in their chairs, seated, with their workout togs on, ready to watch the game film. At about nine-fifteen Shula'd be making his talk; the door would open and in would come this almost indescribable derelict. A lapel would be torn off the suit, the tie would be gone, a day and a half's growth of whiskers, hair all wild, eyes the color of our Volvo out there— not red but burgundy, a sort of crimson color. The suit would

40

be rumpled; obviously he had not been out of it. The good Lord only knows what he'd been doing. There'd be a ripple of laughter through the room; Shula would mark down a twenty-five-dollar fine for being late; the meeting would just go on as if nothing had happened. That was the Hawk. Then toward the end of the meeting Hawk would get up to make his special team award. The award was always a fifth of Cutty Sark Scotch. Every week he'd stand up and he'd say, 'This week Charlie Stukes had a phenomenal performance. He had four tackles on kickoffs and punts. He did a great job overall in everything he was asked to do. Thus the judging was very close, and this is one of the more difficult decisions that I've ever had to make in making the special team award. But the winner again this week, for the twenty-third consecutive week, is Alex Hawkins.'

"Nobody else ever won in all those years! The funny thing about it is that he was usually right. He usually *was* the outstanding performer. He'd make *every* tackle. He'd just go crashing down into the wedge! One week he tore his butt off . . . literally. The hip muscle was disconnected from the pelvis. He came in and the doctor said, 'Oh, my gosh! You've *got* to go directly to the hospital.' Hawk was already shaving, and his old butt was just hanging down! Loose! The muscle was just torn in *half,* already beginning to show ecchymosis—blood discoloration, from blood rupturing into tissues.

"Hawk said, 'Doc, I can't make it.'

" 'I didn't ask you if you could make it! You're going to the hospital. That's a very serious injury.'

"'I'm sorry,' the Hawk said.

"By this time he was pulling on his socks, slapping on his shaving lotion. The doctor said, 'You must not understand what I'm saying to you. I'm your physician and you're going to the hospital.'

" 'I'll tell you what,' the Hawk said. 'We'll make a deal. I'll meet you over there in about three hours. My wife's in town and I've got to see the old lady before I go to the hospital.' He did!

Bless her heart, how she puts up with him I don't know. He got to the hospital about three hours later; they operated. For everybody who went to see him he had a big pitcher of stingers; it was just a drunken three or four days up there at the hospital."

"What's happened to him since?" I asked.

"He became a broadcaster, which was strange because he had an odd, if very lively, way with words. He's the guy who said that the reason Unitas is such a great passer is that he has such remarkable 'perennial vision.' He's also the guy that got put off the air as a CBS analyst for a famous comment about Jake Scott of Miami. Scott had come to the game with two broken hands and, naturally, was having a difficult time, though he was out there trying to play. On national TV Hawkins said, 'And of course, when you've got two broken hands with casts on 'em, and you go to the men's room, that's where you really find out who your friends are.' That's the last word that we heard from the Hawk over the public airwaves for a long time.

"What characters! That was one of the things that made the Colts different. It was just such fun to be there. There was nothing more fun than going to work and getting ready for the next game, and playing the game and winning. We had our clowns, we had our legends, we had our stable influences. Guys like Jerry Logan, who was just a very solid citizen, quiet guy, played good football every Sunday and occasionally he'd make the really big play; we had Bobby Boyd, who was the tactician, who understood the defenses and could impart that to the other guys; Bob Vogel, who was the epitome of the solid German father-influence kind of guy; we had Sam Ball, who was bluegrass, hicksville humor; we had Tom Matte, who's one of the best friends I've ever had, like a brother to me, who would just do whatever he had to do to win the game somehow; he wasn't supposed to be fast enough, but he never realized that. Actually, he had a whole lot more ability than people gave him credit for. In practice, he was usually so busy finding the right blade of grass to slip in the earhole of somebody's helmet to make him jump and cuss the bugs that you failed to notice how hard he was working. He did that to you, didn't he?"

"Continually," I said.

"Well, Matte knew the offense inside and out. That was very fortunate, because Earl Morrall, who had quarterbacked for so many teams that he got his plays mixed up, would come into the huddle and he'd say, 'Okay, let's see . . . let's relax . . . everything's under control . . . out—left—flank—right—split. . . . No, out—right—flank—left? . . . uh . . .' Matte would say, 'Out—left —flank—right 36 on 1,' and we'd break the huddle. Earl'd say, 'Right! That's it; that's it!' "Then when Norm Bulaich came along, Matte blossomed as a great blocker for him. The day Boo gained 198 yards against the Jets, Matte just bombed over their linebackers. He was such a confident person. We *knew* that he was going to produce when he got on the field, and he did."

I found myself staring at the mural. "Do those Indians tell you anything? They look a little Iroquois to me."

"They're wearing sort of togas," Curry observed. "If it weren't for those pipes, they could be Roman senators. Maybe we got the wrong continent." He turned away from the mural. "The great thing about the Colts," he continued, "was that we had so much fun together! We just *enjoyed* it. On Sunday we'd get pretty serious, but even on the sidelines that attitude was there. One day Glenn Ressler, a guard who never said anything, picked up a fumble and took about three steps before six or so Steelers hit him and just about tore him in half. He got up and looked over at Tom Matte, who was beat up from running the ball and complaining about it all the time, and Ressler said, 'There's nothin' to that stuff. Let me try it again. Let me run with the thing!' It was great to hear because Glenn had speed like the tortoise. So it was that attitude of hell-bent-for-leather, but not taking anything too terribly seriously. In fact, Shula had a motto on our team: 'If you can't take a joke, to hell with you.' Of course, every now and then he'd go crazy and start screaming in practice, and either Matte or Hawkins or somebody'd say,

'Hey, Shoes, you can't take a joke!' He'd always laugh. And it was like a magic tension-buster. Of course, you knew certain days when you didn't say it. Dan Sullivan was always our barometer. Sully'd come back to the huddle and say, 'I don't think we're going to kid around with Shoes today.' Yeah, because it would mean it was time to get ready for the Packers or somebody."

I said that I still was not at all clear what the key to the Colts' success was.

Curry shrugged. "People are always asking me what it was about the Colts that had made them superior. Sometimes I said it was the horseshoe. The horseshoe emblem did it. I'm not kidding you. I remember Henry Bullough was a rookie coach with us in 1970, and he got up at the rookie show. He'd had a few beers and he was all worked up. With a tear in his eye, he said something to the effect that there were all types of football teams, but when that headgear with the horseshoe took the field the other team cringed, and that we should all join together in singing the Colt fight song. Upon which he was drowned by about forty pitchers of beer being thrown at him. The *idea* of singing a fight song!

"So it wasn't really a rah-rah kind of thing. It was a bringing together of a unique cast of characters, I know that. There was a kind of mutual-respect factor. It's odd. The cast of characters could change and yet the attitude stayed. I think Carroll Rosenbloom, the owner, had something to do with it—quite a bit, in fact. He built this family atmosphere, and to this day he views himself as a father figure for his players. He always would come around and make an effort to speak to every player. He furnished these marvelous baskets at Thanksgiving time, with a big turkey and a ham and a bottle of champagne and candy for the kids and a little gift for the wife and extra things that weren't really terribly expensive to him, but thoughtful. When a Colt child was born, you'd get a little sterling silver cup with the baby's name engraved on it—that kind of thing—with a Colt emblem. Just bright PR touches, internal. I can't help but think that had a lot to do with it. I don't know if it was done purposefully or not, but if you had trouble negotiating your contract with his general manager, or whoever happened to be negotiating that year, you had the feeling that if you waited until Carroll showed up, you'd end up doing better.

"Of course, he made some mistakes. He made a terrible mistake trading Roy Jefferson, who was such a great wide receiver. Roy's is the kind of personality that won't back down from anybody. A gap developed between him and Rosenbloom. Probably a breakdown in communications, really. But I talked to both of them, and Rosenbloom would say, 'Well, I don't want to trade him, but he's forcing me. Roy would say, 'I don't want to go, but he's forcing me.' Neither one of them would capitulate. It was over a very few dollars, something like a couple of thousand dollars, which, when a player like Jefferson is involved, is not much. So it didn't help us to lose him. In fact, we came within one game of the Super Bowl that year. Didn't make it. We just lacked the punch on offense. Of course, Bulaisch and Matte got hurt that week, too, and we didn't have either one of them.

"But then even the year before it had been touch and go. In 1970 I don't know how many games we won in the last few seconds, but it was several. Unitas'd come in—of course, his track record had a lot to do with it—and there was something about being in a huddle with him with a minute and forty-five seconds left, and you needed a touchdown and you were back on your own twenty-yard line. Everybody'd look over at that famous crooked nose with the scar down it. He sort of blinked his eyes behind the bar on his helmet, and you'd *know* you were going to get a touchdown. And we *would*. It was all so matter-of-fact with him. There was very seldom a pep talk. He might say to Jimmy Orr or Roy Jefferson, 'What ya got? Can you get him on an up? Can you beat him on an out? Is he playing you inside? Okay, let's try it out this time.' He'd stick his head in the huddle and call the play, *boom*. He assumed that we were going to keep a pass rush off of him, and that if we did we were going to win the game. He might say, 'Let's go, keep them out, okay?' It was all very . . . laconic. Just straight forward business. 'Let's go do it. Here we go.'"

"How different were the other quarterbacks?" I asked. "Isn't that businesslike approach very typical?"

"Dan Pastorini with the Oilers was completely different," Curry said. "Very frantic. 'Sons-of-bitches, we gotta score! Now, c'mon! Let's git goin' here! Jeez, c*'mon* now!' He was very young when I was playing with him. Just about every play, somebody's just knocked his head off. He'd be prostrate there, and I'd reach down and help drag him off. He'd be cussing: "Those guys couldn't block my Aunt Suzy. . . .' He really went through hell. He set a couple of NFL records for having been sacked the most times. It was driving him crazy. Now he's doing much better, and I understand he's matured a lot in the huddle.

"They're all a little different. Earl Morrall was almost humorous in his approach. He'd come in the huddle and he'd have a sort of puckish grin on his face. He'd say very slowly and deliberately, 'Okay now, let's calm down. Everything is under control.' Somebody'd say, 'Yeah, Earl, call a play, would ya?' So after a lot of hemming and hawing he'd call a play and we'd win with him.

"Bart Starr was businesslike, like Unitas, though he showed a lot more emotion than John. The common thread of the great ones, of course, was that you had complete confidence in them —that the guy knew which plays to call, and that if you executed them properly it would work. If you had to sit there and wonder: Now, even if we do this and we do it just right, it still might not be the right thing . . . then you'd have a real problem. With the great ones, you did not have to worry. I remember playing in the Pro Bowl one year with Lenny Dawson. Just complete calm—even more so than Unitas. He'd come in the huddle and kneel down. He'd dabble with the grass. He was having a hard time with the system, being new to what Don McCafferty, the coach, had installed. He'd say, 'Bill, what's that split formation?' I'd say, 'Flank split right.' He'd say, 'Oh, yeah, okay. Flank split right.' Then he'd call his play. Complete serenity. We had a big day and beat the National Conference. Each quarterback seems to have his own special kind of presence.

"John Hadl was a snappy, quick play-caller, very rapid-fire. Up to the line, and *boom, boom, boom,* we'd go right in for touchdown. He brought a certain excitement into the huddle; it was electric when he stepped in. Just a complete difference."

The waitress arrived with our coffee. She said she still had not remembered the name of the river. She'd asked her friend Cecile, who took care of tables 3, 4, 5, and 6, and she didn't know.

"We think it's the Tiber," I said.

"I don't remember that one," she said as she headed for the kitchen.

Curry took a sip of his coffee. "Unitas," he said reflectively. "It's always back to him. He provided us with a kind of charisma that I don't think anybody on any of the other teams had . . . at least not to that degree. We could go into an alien environment, in another city, another stadium, against the Houston Oilers or somebody, and when the players were introduced, Unitas would get *such* a roar. Like Notre Dame, the subway alumni . . . We had our own following no matter where we went, and it was all because of him. 'Look, the Baltimore Colts, and that's John Unitas!' We had rooters everywhere. In fact, in the early years of the Falcons in Atlanta, my home town, it was embarrassing to me because we Colts got a *much* bigger hand than the Falcons. If you had to pick one name in the history of the league that helped make it what it is, I don't see how you could come up with anybody other than John Unitas. His presence in the huddle was something extra, too. He had a way of *looking* like a legend when he'd step in there; he'd glare at you if you missed your block, and every now and then he'd say, 'You know whose man that was.' I'd already be mad and upset and I'd say, 'I know whose man it was.' He'd say, 'Well, block him next time.' Well . . . you responded. We called him 'Legend.' 'What'd ya say, Legend?' But it was as much an irreverence, you know. Nobody really cared if he was a legend; nobody treated him like one. Matte constantly goosed him. Unitas was the goosiest man in the world! You'd touch him on his rear end and he'd literally soar up to the ceiling. Just as punchy as he could be. Everything else . . . you'd remember him for his nonchalance, his easygoing manner. I remember at the training camp at Westminster, Maryland, my first year with the Colts. I was sick of practicing football and just kind of depressed . . . lonesome for my family. We were walking over to the meeting and I said, 'John, how're you feeling?' He said, 'Oh, I feel great! Look at that sunshine. Look at that tree. It's great to be alive. You know something? You're a long time dead.' I said, 'What?' He said, 'Yep. You're a long time dead.' I said, 'You know, I guess you're right.' That's his philosophy.

"On the field Unitas had ice water in his veins. Nothing seemed to bother him. With him it was always business as usual. He'd come in, get taped up, and lie down on one of the training tables and go to sleep for fifteen to twenty minutes before a game. If he wasn't asleep, it was a heck of an act. There was just no nonsense about him. It didn't matter whom he was dealing with. I remember in L.A. in 1967 . . . we had not lost a game during the season—thirteen in a row—and we went to the West Coast and got beaten by the Rams, and didn't even make the play-offs. They had an equally good record. I happened to be standing near Unitas when some writer came up and asked, 'Who's going to win the game between the Packers and the Rams next week?' John looked at him and said, 'The team that scores the most points.' Then he walked off. The poor guy's standing there with his pen and his pad. What a thing to ask! We'd just been through a terrible game, and Unitas had not played very well; Roman Gabriel had completed 20 out of 22 or something.

"Like Lombardi with sportswriters: if they asked him stupid questions, he'd sit there almost in disbelief, and he'd give them a stupid answer. Or he would say, 'Gee, that's a stupid question.' Many times I heard Lombardi say, 'Why in the hell would you ask a question like that?' Or he'd laugh, and he'd look around the room at the gathered press corps, and he'd say, 'Now, that's a pisser, isn't it?' Just embarrassed the guy. Or he'd say, 'I'm going to answer that, and I hope to hell you'll write something decent this time. Be creative.'

"After we lost the Super Bowl to the Jets, the press came crowding around Unitas. 'Well, what happened, John? What happened?' He said, 'We got beat.' They pressed on. 'Well, this must be a terrible blow for you after your long and illustrious career. It must be the most painful loss.'

" 'Nope.'

" 'No? Was it the most painful loss?'

" 'I don't feel any pain.'

" 'What d'ya mean?'

" 'I been through too many of these games. It's not a big deal. We lost a game. It's a game!'

"They looked at their pads. 'Does anything upset you?'

"Unitas said, 'Yeah, it'd upset me if somebody'd steal my beer. Then I'd cry.'

"That's exactly what he said."

Chapter 5

"You remember where you were for that game?" Curry asked as we started north again.

"The Super Bowl? You and the Jets? Sure," I said. "I guess it was a day like Bobby Thomson's home run, or Henry Aaron's. I watched with a whole bunch of friends in a New York townhouse, Peter Duchin's, and he set up a pool, I remember, with only one marker for a Jets victory—it was *that* improbable— and Mike, the twelve-year-old son of one of the guests, Tom Guinzburg, pulled it out of the hat and we all commiserated with him and kidded him around. Of course, he had a lot to remember later on that afternoon."

"I don't suppose there'll ever be such a game," Curry said solemnly. "Super Bowl III—the game that brought the two leagues to parity. It made Joe Namath the messiah . . . not only to New Yorkers but to American Football League people everywhere. People in Houston remember that game. Oakland. In fact, very few people *any*where, just like you in New York, will forget what happened. Because on our side of the coin, here we were, the Baltimore Colts, with our great tradition—world champions two years before the Jets were even born. Our record coming into that game was 15 to 1. The only team that had beaten us in the regular season was Cleveland, and when we met them in the NFL title game, we whipped them 34 to 0.

"And then Namath made that blatant and ridiculous prediction that the Jets would beat us. He was playing the only cards he had in his hand—to convince his teammates they had a chance against us. It was a great psychological move. One of the Jets players admitted to me a couple of years later that they had hoped—well, he himself, at any rate—that we wouldn't beat them by more than forty points."

"What do you remember of this *one* game yourself?" I asked. "Can you discuss it?"

Curry laughed. "Hardly," he said. "My personal memory of the game was the steady growth in the self-assuredness of the Jet players from the opening kickoff. When a team is a little bit leery of you, you can see it in their eyes. I don't mean everybody's *afraid* of you; that's not what I mean at all. I just mean that they look a little awed when they come on the field. I know that feeling. Having been with the Packers and Colts for all those years, I know the feeling of being on the superior team; after Houston I knew the feeling of being on an inferior team, and having to try—just as Namath did—to make your teammates believe that they can do what's necessary to win.

"At any rate, the Jets started off kind of wide-eyed, and we were just *ripping* off yardage, running and throwing, and we forced a couple of errors on them, and yet we couldn't capitalize. Every time they'd stop us, you could see their adrenaline pump a little more; you could see the brightness come into the eyes. You could actually *see* this . . . you could *feel* it. The tempo of their hitting picked up as the game turned in their favor.

"There are a couple of things I remember distinctly. . . . The famous flea-flicker play—which we had used earlier in the year to beat the Atlanta Falcons—in which Earl Morrall would hand off to Tom Matte, who would start a sweep to his right; meanwhile Earl would drift back out to the left, behind Matte, so that Tom could turn and throw him a lateral back across the field. While all this was going on, Jimmy Orr was sneaking off thirty yards from the nearest defender . . . waiting for Earl's pass. We'd only run it a couple of times and it had worked. My job on the play was to block back into the defensive tackle, who in this case was John Elliott. Of course, he would read the run—the sweep to the right—and begin to pursue. As he slipped off, I was supposed to slide out as a personal protector for the quarterback once he got Tom's long lateral. What I remember about the play is as I was running out there—and you're not supposed to do this—I sneaked a look downfield and I saw Jimmy just standing in the end zone as if he were waiting for a bus in the rain and I had that warm feeling: Well, we've done it to 'em again and this is gonna get us back in the game 'cause it's a sure touchdown . . . you know how quickly things can run through your mind, especially when your senses are very sharp and heightened in a pressure situation. About that time I looked up and here came Elliott. He had read the sweep but, with his great hustle, he had been the first one back out toward Earl. So I hit John Elliott with a block as Earl threw the ball. And here, again, the story is pretty well known. Earl, for reasons unknown to him or anybody else, didn't look at Jimmy, though Orr was really the only receiver on the play, supposedly, except for Jerry Hill, the fullback, who was a safety valve just in case, sort of trailing down the middle. And Earl threw to *him*. Even Jerry was open. But it was a poor throw and the ball was intercepted. I remember that distinctly. But the dismay that runs through you at a time like that is usually offset by the determination that you're going to get the ball back. That's exactly the way I felt —until there were four seconds left in the game. I *swear* I knew *somehow* we were going to win that game.

"When we were down 16 to 0, with seven or eight minutes

left, John Unitas was sent in—with a torn arm muscle; he had played very little that year. I don't know why we expected him to be anything but . . . John. But as he joined us in the huddle in that critical situation, somehow you half expected him to say something terribly dramatic, like: 'All right, men, we are the Baltimore *Colts* from the NFL; let's handle ourselves accordingly and *win* this football game.' Something like that. What do you think he said? He came jogging into the huddle, looked around, and he said, 'Okay, we gotta get two touchdowns and a field goal quick here. Let's do it.'

"One of the things I remember about the last part of the game is Tommy Bell, the referee. He is really the only referee who has ever stuck out in my mind. The rest of them are faces; they'll come up and say, 'Hello, Bill, how ya doing?' But Tommy Bell is interesting because he builds a relationship with every team. The first time I really noticed him was in 1968 when we were playing the Bears, and they were just taking cheap shots. . . . One of the few times that I've seen Tommy's team of officials let a game begin to get out of hand. I began screaming, 'You can't let them get away with this crap! They've just been doing this all day and they're going to keep right on doing it.' Bell's about five foot seven; he stepped right up to me and said, 'Not with Tommy here.' So I was always aware of him after that and I noticed that his team of officials called most of the big games. . . .

"When there was about a minute left in the Super Bowl and it was pretty obvious we were going to lose, he came over and stuck his head in the huddle during a time-out. He said, 'Now, men, you're champions. Let's finish this game like champions and leave the field with your head high.' There were beginning to be a few fisticuffs and kicking. Oh, yeah, we were upset. That's when people really start to get in fights. But that was his way of calming us down.

"Finally, on the playing field itself, the last thing I remember is seeing Joe Namath as he turned and jogged off through the crowd in that famous pose, holding up the one finger, not in a lewd gesture, but indicating number one for the Jets.

"There we were, the 'greatest team in the history of the NFL,' representing fifty years of tradition, with that damn record of 15 to 1, and we'd just finished the only game that would be remembered. When the press came into the locker room, many of them headed for my locker. I had been in the first Super Bowl with the Green Bay Packers, then missed the second, having gone to the Colts, and was now playing in the third —the only player from the NFL who had been in two of the first three. So they had made a big thing of it—especially in respect to a comparison of the coaching techniques and methods of Don Shula of the Colts and Lombardi of the Packers. Since I had come out in favor of Shula—most of it accurately and extensively reported—the writers crowded around, wanting to hear what the . . . the blowhard, I guess, was going to say after the debacle against the Jets. I didn't disappoint them at all. Instead of being gracious or humble in defeat, whichever one of those things it is you're supposed to be, I was really chafing . . . because never have I been, nor will I ever be again, affected so dramatically and traumatically by an athletic event. I was accepting this as disastrous an event as a death in the family. When they came in to ask me about the Jet team, I told them exactly what I thought. I still feel this way, but let's just say it isn't smart to speak out . . . especially when you're tired and emotionally drained and so disappointed. I said the Jets were one of . . . oh, probably maybe the *sixth* best team we had played that year, and there was absolutely no way they would beat us again if we played ten times. Something to that effect. And it got a big play the next day, from what I hear. I don't know. I didn't read the articles. I was only able to hold together emotionally—which is unusual for me—until I got outside the dressing room, and right there in front of my family, of all things, I just . . . well, I didn't break down and go to pieces, you may be surprised to hear, but I really choked up."

54

"What did you do that evening?" I asked.

"Carroll Rosenbloom had a party at his house at Golden Beach—one of the real disasters. Senator Edward Kennedy was there, Burt Lancaster, other celebrities, and people who had come to see Mr. Rosenbloom win his third world championship. We just looked at each other, all of us . . . indescribably gloomy faces trying to act like it really wasn't that big a deal. Mr. Rosenbloom made the rounds, and so far as I could tell, tried to speak to each player. I remember him walking up to me and saying, 'Well, Bill, it's just impossible to believe or accept, isn't it?' I remember exactly what I said: 'Mr. Rosenbloom, it'll never happen again; we'll be back, because there are too many good players on this team.' Fortunately, two years later I was able to remind him of that at a victory party in Miami.

"But at the time, after the game, I receded into a shell. I've only done it once before, and that was after having been let go by the Packers. I didn't answer the phone, I didn't read the papers, I didn't go to work. I didn't do anything. I just concentrated on feeling sorry for myself, and I became very proficient at it. Naturally there was great derision from every corner. The NFL players resented us for making them look bad. And the AFL players were just gleeful. One particular incident stands out in my mind . . . when I ran into an AFL player, Billy Shaw, at the airport one night during the off-season. Billy Shaw was a great guard for the Buffalo Bills for many years; he was a graduate of Georgia Tech, who had been a senior and a captain of the Tech team in my freshman year. He had always been very pleasant and extremely nice to me through the years. At the airport we chatted—small talk, you know, the usual amenities —and then suddenly this complete change took over in his appearance and his demeanor, and he said, 'Well, after that Super Bowl game, I guess you guys are going to finally respect us. The big shots have been brought down.' There was great bitterness in his voice. It hurt my feelings because I had never said anything about that league.

"From the economic standpoint, the loss probably cost us about ten to twelve thousand dollars per player. For years we were subjected to the Jets on television, in commercials, on the printed page, smiling at us, singing, washing, shaving, eating soup, standing alongside cars, wearing sports clothes. The most obnoxious by far was one in which Gerry Philbin was shown eating Manhandlers soup, whatever *that* was, just stuffing his face with it like he was never going to have another meal in his life. Every time we turned around, our shame—our economic deprivation—was hammered at us.

"Why, the morning after the game, in a taxicab trying to get out of town as fast as possible with my family, the cabby looked back. 'You one them Colt players?'

" 'Yep.'

" 'You guys cost me twenty bucks yesterday.'

"I wanted to pull him out from behind the steering wheel and throttle him."

"How long did that go on?" I asked.

"It was incessant," Curry replied, "and brutal. I didn't know at the time that the taxicab experience was just the smallest taste of what I was going to get for the rest of the season. There was one guy in a bar in Brunswick, Georgia. It's the closest I've ever come to physically . . . not assaulting, but 'helping' a fellow leave a bar. He came up to me after I'd spoken at a banquet down there. I was with some friends. He said, 'Bill Curry?' 'Yep.' This is months after the game! He said, 'I just want to tell you one thing. You guys really hurt a *lot* of people around here in Georgia. I want you to know that!' He said it with such venom that I really wanted to cuff him around. Instead I said, 'Don't even *talk* to me about it hurting. Do you understand that!' I don't know if that scared him or what; he didn't come back over; didn't come near me again. I mustered my most baleful Sonny Liston stare, because I was deadly serious.

"Later on I went to Alaska, which is—what?—four thousand or five thousand miles from here, to speak for the Air Force at the Nike missile bases. Those guys sit up there in those hills watching for Russian missiles for a solid year, and they really don't get to come down very much. I think I made fourteen speeches at various bases, traveling on every kind of flying contraption—from the most modern helicopter to an airplane made the same year I was. I laid my best lines on 'em, and we'd show the Super Bowl film, and I'd stand there for the question-and-answer period . . . and *every single place that we went,* all over that huge state which stretches from the tip of the Aleutians to the easternmost point, the same distance as from Los Angeles to Savannah, Georgia—every single place we went in that vast terrain the question was the same: *'What happened?'*

"It *was* so hard to believe, but some of the conjectures got ugly . . . unbelievable. Every year there's a very nice function at a place called the Center Club in Baltimore. My line when I was invited to speak the first time was that I thanked them for naming their club after me. It's a very exclusive place, right at the top of the Charles Center building . . . very plush and nice, and you take your wives, and then the guys stand up, and we would all make asses of ourselves.

"Tom Matte and I were standing over on one side of the room; a guy came over. You can always tell when it's going to be one of those venomous jobs because they've got this smirk on their face and they've had a couple of drinks and their tongue's loose and they're very brave. He said, 'You two guys come over here a minute. I want to talk to you.' So Tom and I walked over, and you know how friendly Tom is: 'Yeah, nice to see you. How are you? Yes, I remember you from the last year.' This guy says, 'I just want to know one thing. I don't want any crap. I want the truth and I want it now!' Then he turns and calls one of his friends over. 'Hey, come on over here, George. I want you to hear this!' He was really enjoying himself. Tom and I, we're beginning to look at each other. This guy said, 'Now, I want you two to tell me *how* and *why* you threw that football game to the Jets!'

"Well, at first, even though we knew the guy was serious, we smiled at each other, like: Okay, wonder how long we'll have to stand here. But then he got adamant. 'Listen, I'm not kidding around with you guys. I wanta know! I've got to know *why* you did it. I've been a Colt fan for all these years and I live and die with you guys, and you go out there and you *throw* that game. I know you got paid off. Now tell me about it! Tell me what you got!'

"Well, I had to take Tom by the arm because he would . . . well, he would've decked him, and of course we would've gained nothing by that. We turned and walked away from him. Fortunately, he didn't pursue.

"That sort of thing kept up in varying degrees—lots of people telling me that I had lost ten bucks for them. My banker—a good friend of mine—called me into his office and asked me why I and the rest of the offensive line had played such a poor game . . . when in fact the offensive line had probably had its best game of the year. The Jets didn't tackle our quarterback once; we averaged six yards a carry, running the ball. That didn't make any difference. Everybody else was an authority after that.

"Every time I'd get into confrontations like that, I kept thinking—just little quick mental images—of Rick Volk, our safety, and what had happened to him that afternoon. Early in the game Matt Snell came off tackle, as he did all day, and he came clear in the secondary. Big, powerful churning legs. Rick came up and met him head to head. Just a tremendous smash! When Rick got up he couldn't stand straight; he wobbled around like Ray Bolger's Straw Man in *The Wizard of Oz*. It would have been comical except we knew he was hurt bad. They got him over to the sidelines, where he stayed, I think, for a couple of quarters. Then late in the game we tried an on-side kick . . . which is just created for someone like Rick, with his agility and quick reflexes, to recover. So he went back into the game and *he got the ball*, recovering it, but as he did so, somebody hit him on the head. So he was gone again. When we got to the locker room there was Rick laid out on the table. Didn't know where he was, or anything. Still, we went over to console him and try to talk to him. It's part of the ritual. Then you forget about it, because all of us get hurt like that. You figure you'll see him the next morning and he'll be fine.

"Well, we rode back to the hotel, and as we were walking into the lobby to go upstairs and change clothes for Carroll Rosenbloom's 'victory' party, a stretcher was carried out of the elevator banks with Rick on it. He was vomiting—vomiting blood, I might add. His wife, Charlene, was walking alongside, crying. We helped carry him out to the ambulance, and afterward we went over and sat with Charlene in the hospital for a couple of hours while they examined him. Finally they came out and said he was going to be fine after a couple of days of rest. But I kept thinking about that sort of sacrifice listening to buffoons ask me about throwing the Super Bowl game.

"Do you remember Dmitri Spassoff? He was an old Bulgarian trainer we had with the Colts . . . very heavy accent, and he was always telling us about 'my son John.' In fact, that's what we nicknamed him—My Son John. 'You seen My Son John around anywhere?' He was always talking about the 'Thirteenth Commandment' and how important it was, more important than the other ten—I don't know *how* he got to thirteen!—and of course somebody in the training room would eventually bite: 'Okay, My Son John, what's the Thirteenth Commandment?'

"He'd say, 'Don't take yourself too damn serious. Dat is the most important commandment in all duh world! In all your life, dat is the most important.'

"He may be right. But I keep thinking back on that game. What could have happened? Maybe it was bad to bring the families down. The girls came down in the middle of the week —just at the most intense part of our preparations. Suddenly it was like being on a big holiday. The girls went out shopping. Carolyn bought a bathing suit that was just perfect for a forty-five-year-old lady; she came in and tried it on and I told her what I thought of it. So we had one of our spats. I didn't need that. Kids were everywhere. Fanny Logan got sick as a dog and Jerry had to take care of her. He didn't sleep the night before the game.

"So the next Super Bowl, we stayed out away from Miami Beach at the Miami Lakes Country Club, where there was nothing to do . . . and the families didn't come down until the night before the game and then they were put somewhere else. And we still played terrible! Against the Cowboys, though we did win the game. Utterly baffling how you can get to the biggest game of the year—biggest game of your life!—and go out there and not be *prepared.* I will never understand. People ask me, 'How do you prepare for the Super Bowl? You've been in so many of them.' Of the four championship games I've played in, the two when I played with the Packers we were ready, and the two that I played with the Colts we simply weren't . . . though we managed to win one of those anyhow. I should be accurate. Against the Cowboys the defense was ready, and that's the only reason we won. But the offense had eight turnovers. Terrible, dumb things happening *all* through the game . . . even a lot of things that nobody would know except me and the rest of the offensive line. There must be some secret to getting ready for a Super Bowl or a big game, but I don't know what it would be. Hard work wasn't enough. Nor concentration. Our practices were excellent both times. Really still bugs me a lot. Really does. When I'm thinking football, or talking football, I keep picking at it. Why? Why?"

Chapter 6

Curry's career in the NFL certainly had its crises—not only the Super Bowl game against the Jets, but those that happened because as a player who liked to be involved, he was very much affected by the fortunes of the teams he was with, and with the personnel he got to know. I had always thought that the most anguishing time must have been when the Baltimore Colts, that happy band, started to disintegrate after Joe Thomas, the new general manager, turned up and began to clear house ostensibly to create a team of his own making. When Don McCafferty, the coach, was fired, Curry wrote a strong, emotional statement in which he absolved the coach of blame, rebuked the team for its play and the front office for its decision. At a meeting he tried to get the team to stand behind his statement, but they wouldn't. A watered-down statement was issued . . . and Thomas must have felt quite secure in going ahead and doing what he wished to do.

We got to talking about that strange time, as we moved north through the Indiana fields. I asked Curry if it was easy to diagnose the problem with the Colts—the beginning of the collapse.

"Lord, yes," Curry said. "The Colts began to dissolve with the change in ownership. Even if people weren't endeared by Carroll Rosenbloom, they knew that he was competent; he knew what he was doing; he was most anxious for us to win and people knew he would do darned near anything to help us. What Rosenbloom and his general manager, Don Klosterman, did very well—whatever faults they may have had—was that they related well and engendered a feeling of family. When the team changed hands we didn't see the new owner, Bob Irsay; we didn't see the new general manager, Joe Thomas; we didn't know who they were except by name for weeks after we got to the training camp down in Tampa, Florida. Finally, when Bob Irsay did show up, he only talked to the team for about thirty seconds; he was painfully shy and very uneasy around us, which made us uneasy. I'm not trying to lay the blame at his feet. I'm just saying that it was one contributing factor. That's what began the deterioration. Then we had a number of serious injuries. We lost Bubba Smith for the year. Norm Bulaich could not stay healthy. Matte was injured, our other starting running back. We lost John Williams in a trade to Los Angeles. We had a 1 and 4 record after five games of the season."

"What do you do when something like that happens?" I asked.

"We tried to live it up and be happy," Curry replied. "It was like old times, and we were going to have a good football team. Coach McCafferty kept telling us, 'Dadgummit, we've got a good team. We're the same group that the year before last won the Super Bowl and almost went last year. Let's get it together. We're going to be all right.' But always, *always* loomed this ominous specter of Joe Thomas. I don't know any other way to say it. So Coach McCafferty was unceremoniously dumped, with absolutely no concern for his feelings or his dignity; Unitas was unceremoniously benched. Whether or not the decision was right to bench him, the way it was done was a problem for all of us. What enthusiasm there was began to dissolve, replaced by 'false chatter,' sort of hollering but you don't mean anything by it at all. Instead of concentrating on our jobs, we were worried about what was going on in management. We began to feel sorry for ourselves and for our teammates and for our departed coach. You just can't win if you're doing that. And we didn't.

"Eight days after the Pro Bowl game which ends the season I picked up the phone and called Joe Thomas's office. He was not there, so I left a message. A few minutes later the phone rang, and Joe was returning my Operator 6 call-back. He was telephoning me on my nickel, which is neither here nor there—two or three bucks for the phone call is incidental—but he called me back on *my* nickel to say, 'Bill, I guess you've heard about the trade.' I said, 'No.' He said, 'Over the weekend we traded you to the Houston Oilers.' And he began to laugh.

"He got rid of twenty-three of the best players in the world. One can only surmise that he wanted his own people in there . . . that the team would be a Joe Thomas creation.

"One of the players he traded was Ray May. He's worth talking about. He was one of the most extraordinary Colts—in a way he typified the Colt tradition I've been talking about. You remember him, don't you?"

"Boy, do I!" I said, laughing. "He dislocated my thumb. . . . Picked me up in one of those one-on-one nutcracker drills and threw me into the ground like a spear."

"You stuck there and quivered."

"Damn near. He came to my room that evening, where I was sitting with my thumb bandaged up, and he said he was sorry that he'd put me in the repair shop—'Didn't mean to jack you up' was the way he put it."

"Well, he almost destroyed me the first time I played against him," Curry said. "He came into the NFL with the Steelers and in that game he made nineteen tackles. Just destroyed me! I couldn't believe how good he was. I went and found him after the game and I told him that I thought he was excellent. When I found out we had traded for him two years later, I was delighted. We got to know each other. He comes from Los Angeles, and though I don't think he ever lived in poverty, he certainly knew what it meant to be in a troubled area. His parents taught him from the outset by good example; if he brought home a hungry kid, his mother would just take him in. Some of them ended up being literally adopted, becoming members of the family. So for Ray it was just a matter of that's the way you treat people in trouble. As an adult he spent his off-season in Los Angeles working at a playground and when he would see kids skipping school—cutting class—he'd force them into his car and take them back. He was a sort of unofficial truant officer. Then he began to run across a kid every now and then whose parents didn't even want him around. So Ray would take him in, and he ended up with an endless procession of kids whom he fed, dressed, and sent to school. One year he paid eleven thousand dollars in college tuition for some kid, out of his pocket. He gets them into school, he finds scholarships where he can; he finds schools that are interested in helping out. He's just really an incredible person. I once asked him on a television program how he had come to that tremendous level of commitment. He said, 'Well, number one, I had the advantage of having been raised that way. I don't know if you'd call it an advantage, but it's just the way I view things. I like to try to help. Number two, we're closing in on a time in this country when you're really not going to have a choice anymore. Everybody's going to have to get involved; everybody's going to have to love somebody. It's almost a matter of necessity. The more I can do, the better.' That's the sort of person he is, and there's absolutely no strings attached, no phoniness. He was traded to the Denver Broncos, and the next thing you know, the Denver Broncos were holding hands in the defensive huddle, something Ray got them to do to give them a sense of being a unit.

64

Everybody chuckled about it until they tried to run the ball on them, and suddenly their defense was swarming all over the place. There's one reason: Ray May. . . .

"Well, after Joe Thomas had cleaned out a lot of us, he called in Ray May and he said, 'Look, I want you to be my leader.' Ray said, 'If you want to change the attitude on this team and have us regain our respect for each other and the kind of love we had before, I'll work with you.' Thomas replied, 'All that love and respect stuff is a myth. That doesn't exist. You win football games with quality players and execution; you don't need that crap. What I'm talking about is I want some leadership from you.' Ray said, 'No, thank you.' Thomas told him that he would adjust his contract. Ray turned him down at every turn. He said, 'You can just send me on out of here, because I can't play the way you're talking.'

"This went on through the exhibition season and into several weeks of the league season. Ray would call me in Houston three nights a week at midnight. He'd wake me up and he'd say, 'You've got to get me out of here. I'm going crazy. Did you talk to those people at Houston?' I said, 'Yeah, I talked to Sid Gillman today.' Every day I'd go to see him and say, 'Ray May is anxious and we need him and he can be great for us.' Gillman, who was general manager, was trying to get him, but he couldn't.

"Finally Ray just started doing things at practice. They would call a man-to-man coverage and he would blitz. They'd call a blitz, and he'd do a man-to-man. He packed his van up. He has a big van, and he packed it with all his clothes and all his belongings and he drove it to Memorial Stadium and he slept in it at night. The coaches would come to practice, or Thomas would come in in the morning. He'd say, 'What are you doing here?' 'I'm just ready. I'm ready to go. Where are you sending me? I'll leave today.' He said that to Thomas every single day.

"Finally, of course, they traded him. They'd put him on the kickoff coverage team to teach him a lesson. He told me, 'Bill,

I came down the field so slowly I didn't even show up on the film. I wasn't in the wave. I was behind the camera field.'

"Well, you take a guy with tremendous pride like Ray May's and cause him to feel like he has to do something like *that*, and there's something wrong with your operation. Of course, at that time there *was* something seriously wrong with the operation. But Ray's gone to Denver and he's done extremely well. He's formed a foundation—I think it's called the Rocky Mountain Boys Camps. He's got some land out there, and he's still working with these youngsters. He's the kind of person that I could stop right up here at Thornton, Indiana—is that what the sign said?—and pick up the phone and say, 'Ray, I need you here in Thornton,' and he wouldn't even ask me why; he would just show up in a few hours. And I would do the same for him."

Chapter 7

We drove past the town of Lafayette, Indiana—the name up on the green expressway overhang—and Curry exclaimed:

"Lafayette! Hey, this is where Carolyn and I stayed after we won the NFL championship against Cleveland in 1965. Muddy, snowy day. Ray Nitschke had a big afternoon against Jim Brown. Carolyn and I packed our car the day before and we left right after the game; we couldn't wait to get home. Right here in Lafayette is where we stayed that night. I guess we were the happiest we'd ever been, because we had just learned we were going to have our first child. Carolyn was about two months pregnant, and it had just been confirmed by the doctor. Well, driving on down, we got to the Kentucky line, and she began to have a miscarriage. We ended up making it home, but the doctor had to put her in a hospital, and so it became a very sad time. About a year later Kristin came along, so everything was all right. But it was here in Lafayette that we celebrated right after the championship game."

"What did you do?" I asked. "Is it a good town for celebrating?"

"We had two Coca-Colas and a Seven-Up," Curry replied with a grin. "I'm sure we had nothing more than that. At that time neither of us believed in any form of alcoholic beverage. Up in Green Bay I was adamant on the subject. There had been a worldwide study conducted in which it was learned that Wisconsin placed third, behind Luxembourg and Germany, in per capita consumption of beer. To tell anyone from Wisconsin that you don't drink beer is like saying you don't drink water. People would offer me a beer. I'd say, 'No, thank you.' 'Come on, have a barley pop.' 'I'll have a Seven-Up.' They thought we were crazy."

I said that I had not remembered him as being especially abstemious during my time with the Colts. Curry grinned and said that when he got perambulating around the NFL, his habits changed. "I don't think I could have survived in Kerrville, Texas, without the thought of a cool beer to get me through the day. No wonder Thomas laughed when he sent me there."

"Kerrville?"

"That's where the Oilers train," Curry said. "It's known as the deer-hunting capital of the nation. They're everywhere. At night we could drive out into those beautiful parks and stop the car to watch the deer walk out into the beams of the headlights. Fifteen deer would come out and stand transfixed. It's lush-looking country, but oddly the soil itself is gray and parched and has a sterile look to it . . . cracked. Centers get physically involved with the earth, so we remark on this sort of thing. I could see the trees and the rolling hills, and yet down in my stance, expecting dark, loamy soil, it was like cement, and it's hard to understand where the plant life gets its sustenance. There are hills of fire ants on the practice field. So the ground is inhospitable. But at practice you see the deer in the fields across the way, almost like the plains of Africa, and they look over and watch us.

"We worked in dry, windy days, which made it comfortable even though the temperatures were high. But then sometimes the wind would stop; it would just shut down and it was like being in a sauna bath. The contrast was so marked that I'd wake up with a kind of dread fear that it might be one of those still days.

"Another contrast was the one between the very religious atmosphere in the community, with a lot of emphasis on God, country, and all the things that go along with the Bible Belt ethic, and on the other hand, a racial bigotry much more blatant than it was in Atlanta when I was a kid. There was really a delightful place called Cryder's where they had a rodeo every Saturday night, and after the rodeo a sort of square dance. Just what you'd expect to find in Texas, with a lot of gaiety. One night Billy Parks and Tody Smith and Ron Saul decided they'd go to Cryder's. Ron and Billy are white. Tody is Bubba's younger brother and is black. Ron walked up to the gate and said he'd like three tickets. The guard looked at him and said, 'Well, you can have one and he can have one'—he indicated Billy. But he looked at Tody and said, 'He can't come in.' Ron started to make a big fuss about it, but Tody just restrained him and said he understood. As a team, we decided none of us would go back to Cryder's, but it was no great blow to their business.

"Once we were at a baseball game between the Kerrville Indians and the Arlington Plumbers—I'm not kidding, that was their name—when this old fellow sitting down in front of us in the wooden stands turned around and asked, 'Who do you think is more valuable: white man, nigger, or Mexican?' I said, 'Well, gee . . .' He went ahead to say, 'I tell you who's valuable: nigger worth eleven dollars a pound; white man worth nineteen dollars a pound; Mexican worth twenty-three dollars a pound.' I don't know where this figuring came from, but it was part of the creepy mentality of the place.

"We trained at a school called the Shriner Institute. Utterly quiet. It's a private high school, and being the summer, there were no students. Just football players. Sometimes I'd hear a guy snoring way down the hall, the squeak of a bedspring as someone turned. This one morning, at six forty-five—I remember the time because I was so astonished I looked at my watch —a huge high school band began to practice on the lawn outside our dormitory . . . they just *burst* into their music. Sousa march. I looked out and saw a band director on a platform with his bullhorn—and out in front of him a 175-piece group practicing for a half-time show at some high school game with their tubas and bass drums and the rest of it . . . majorettes throwing their batons up. They came out periodically, getting into position as quiet as deer on the lawn, aiming all those instruments at the dormitory windows, and then *boom!*

"The worst time of training there at the Shriner Institute was going out for the afternoon practice. It'll be the same at Green Bay—my most unfavorite time of the day . . . already through one miserable workout, and now about to go through another . . . groggy, almost dazed . . . and during two-a-days I always had a headache . . . usually dull, but occasionally it became searing.

"When I was a kid, we went swimming at the Y. Sometimes the big guys would duck us, pushing our heads under the water, and when we came up, they'd splash water in our faces and push us under again. But we were gluttons for punishment. I guess it was getting attention from the older ones . . . and so it was okay if they wanted to do these things. We would accept it for hours! I just can't imagine why! I always came out with red eyes, and a throbbing, lingering headache. That's what training camp feels like—like there's water in your head; it sloshes and you can hear it in your skull.

"As we'd come out in front of the dorm for the afternoon practice it would be about ninety-eight degrees and cloudless and members of the high school band that had blasted us out of our beds at dawn would be playing football. It was the 'shirts' against the 'skins,' and it brought back so many memories of when football was *really* fun. The plays were called with fervor and conscientiousness, with the good catches and runs rewarded with cheering and exaggerated hand-slapping and the pats on the butts . . . all that sort of thing. The kids were really having a joyous experience. And here I was, that sloshing feeling in my head, going over to participate in the same game, me, thirty-one years of age, high salary, family responsibilities, college degree, keen mind, broken nose, eloquence, ambition and foolish ego—I was going over to play the same game . . . and yet, I was miserable. I kept wondering: What have we done? What have we done with this game?

"Of course, at Kerrville with the Oilers it was very easy to form doubts. I had become a part of an organization that had no formal organizational chart that functioned, no real chain of command. Bud Adams owned the team. Sid Gillman was the general manager and eventually became coach, taking over from Bill Peterson, who was the coach when I got there. None of them seemed to get along with each other, and Peterson, the head coach, was new to pro-ball and had trouble communicating with the players."

"Peterson?" I asked.

"Bill Peterson. He was a big, ruggedly handsome guy. He liked to smoke big cigars, which he chewed on nervously and vigorously; there were little tobacco specks on his chin and shirt. His career started at Florida State when they were *nothing.* He went on to put together an astounding coaching record. He was picked to coach the Oilers, his first professional job.

"On the first day I came to the training camp at Kerrville, Peterson asked me as a veteran to help him. He took me aside and he said, 'Bill, I'm going to talk to the team about being together and caring about one another.'

" 'Well, that's great, Pete,' I said. 'I happen to be a strong believer in those things.'

"So he asked, 'Well, if you were making the talk, what would you say?'

" 'Well, I would talk about the fact that in any team effort, the inner resolve that motivates in times of stress comes from . . . to a large extent from loyalty; that one must be loyal to his teammates.'

"He looked at me, and I went on about a hundred-degree temperature in the fourth quarter and looking over at my teammate and seeing him sweatin' and bleedin', and knowing that he's hurt and understanding that we all had to care about each other if we expected to perform as a unit. I said that all this was really the justification for having this game. Well, to my amazement, he walked up in front of the team that night and he said, 'Men, we've got to care about each other, and in the fourth quarter when you look over at your teammate and he's sweatin' and bleedin', then that should motivate you; we've got to *care* about each other, and that's the justification for this business.' He quoted me just about verbatim.

"Just before we played our first exhibition game against the Bears, he named Elvin Bethea and me captains, and we went out for the coin toss before the start of the game. As I came jogging back onto the sidelines, I had the odd feeling of being a stranger in the midst of people I didn't know—everyone was looking around bewildered—when the group should have been humming with tension, and Peterson stared at me and he said, 'Bill, tell us something!' So I said, 'Oh. Uh, men, we've got a job to do tonight. We've got a team to play, so let's go play'— something *really* profound like that. He caught me so completely off guard.

"Well, we lost the game 16 to 13, and as we were going off the field, Peterson called out to me as I was walking up the rampway to the locker room, and he called out, 'Curry, what do you say to a team like this after you lose a game?' I said, 'Well, you tell them this is just an exhibition game and we're going to correct some of those errors. And not to worry too much about it.' I went on: 'The thing *not* to do with a young club is to panic —either as a coaching staff or as a squad. The fact that we're putting together a new outfit here means that we may have to work harder than the other clubs.'

"So with that, Pete stood up in front of the club and he said, 'We're not going to panic. We're going to work *twice* as hard as anybody else; he said this in great heat.

"Yes. Imagine Vince Lombardi walking up to a player and asking him what he should say to a team. Lombardi came into the locker room after a loss my rookie year—to the Bears—and he said, 'Men, now I've got something to sink my teeth into— *you!*' When he said it, it made your skin crawl because you had the feeling that he might. That was one of thousands of things he did to teach you that he was in absolute control. But at Houston all these subtle little nuances suggesting a lack of control began to build up—not just on me, but on the team—until finally there was a complete deterioration of confidence in everything that was going on. When we finally beat Dallas in a preseason game, everybody was shouting and acting as jubilant as if we'd won the Super Bowl . . . pounding each other's shoulders as we walked up the ramp. But again Peterson called me over and he asked me, 'What should I say?'

" 'Pete,' I said, 'tell 'em a new day's dawning.'

"Well, he walked into the locker room, pulled up a chair to stand on, and he shouted for the attention of the team. 'Men! Men! Listen to me! I want to just tell you one thing: A new day's dawning!' He raised his fists in the air. A great shout went up from the fifty or sixty guys in the room, and this tremendous goose-pimply type of camaraderie began to grow. But as I sat there I just sank a little deeper into my concern about what was going to happen.

"Poor Pete. There were extraordinary stories about Pete. One involved—I heard it from several reliable sources—the pregame prayer when he was the head coach at Florida State. He gathered his team around him. 'All right, men.' He bowed his head and began to lead the team in prayer. He started off, 'Now I lay me down to sleep, I pray the Lord my soul . . .' and then he caught himself—hell, he was probably wondering who to start at offensive tackle—and realized what he was doing. On his team was a very religious kid, Bobby Somebody-or-other, who was the son of a minister, and the speculation was that he intended to go into the ministry. Peterson happened to catch sight of him. 'Take it away, Bobby!' he called out. Poor Bobby. He started and mumbled a few words, improvising a quickie prayer to get the team ready with the Lord for the game.

"What were his assistants like?" I asked.

"There were some good pros," Curry replied. "Lew Carpenter. He was the most versatile player Lombardi ever had at Green Bay . . . fullback, halfback, tight end, wide receiver, and even quarterback. He would come back behind the huddle out there at the Houston practices and he'd say, 'What do you think the old man would say about this?' He'd shake his head and say, 'I can't believe it.' The most memorable of the coaches was the offensive line coach, Joe Madro. He played for Ohio State in the thirties, and he's five foot six. He smokes incessantly and nervously. He has a ruddy complexion; goes around without a shirt, and for all the world, walks like a bantam rooster. His hair is graying, and it's combed back. Constant cigarette, and to make matters more incongruous, he smokes these Benson & Hedges that are about seven inches long, so that in his hand the cigarette looks like he's got a swagger stick, except that he drags on it constantly. Sometimes he'll have two or three lit up, sitting around in different places. He'll put one down and forget it and light up another. He talks . . . a constant flow of a li'l Shakespeare here, li'l bullshit there. He wears black coaching shoes with the ridges on the bottoms, which are actually elevator shoes, so he kind of squeaks when he walks. On the field, he loves to give demonstrations. He'll get Tody Smith or John Matuszak in front of him, and against these enormous men he looks exactly like Tom Thumb. He gets his chin up and he's humping and hitting up at these guys, and they're just standing there, and though he knew what he was talking about and was a proficient technique instructor, it's all we could do to keep from going into hysterics.

"Communicating with us, he used hundreds of little phrases, *bon mots,* quips, thoughts-for-the-moment, sayings by which he hoped to impress us and teach us. He quite often said about himself, 'I'm not anything but a high-priced teacher. That's all a coach is—a high-priced teacher.' The trouble was that it became intimidation rather than instruction, obsessive rather than natural. He was a crazy sort of stickler about the language and how it should be spoken. One day I asked him a question: 'Now if he was coming at me—'

"Joe cried out, 'Were! Were! If he *were* coming at you . . .' and then he quoted me the rule, right through. He hated people to say 'Right.' If he asked me, 'Now, Curry, do you understand that you block back on that play?' and I replied, 'Right,' he'd say, 'No. *Correct. Right* is a direction.' He was always catching players off guard with these things, and he'd grin this little puckish smile. Anytime anybody called out to him, 'Hey, Joe!' he'd respond, 'Hay? That makes me homesick for the farm.'" It wasn't very funny the first time we heard it—especially to the guy who called out 'Hey, Joe!'—and it didn't improve on hearing it ten times, which we did.

"A black guy'd hold up his hand in class and say, 'Joe, let me aks you a question.' Joe would say, 'What do you mean? You don't have an ax; how are you going to ax me a question? What're you going to do—chop wood? You may *ask* me a question. I'll be glad to answer it for you.' He just wouldn't tolerate any bad English . . . and of course the black guys took it as an insult.

"We had a Chinese center, a rookie named Ron Lou, who came from Arizona and grew up in Los Angeles. We think of Chinese and Japanese as small people, but Ron Lou's about six two and 235. Well built. Perhaps he has a little Polish locked in along with the Chinese, because when he makes a mistake he gets up off the ground and hits himself on the front of the head with the heel of his palm. That old Polish joke. He's very nervous; he throws up. The only other guy I remember that threw up before every game was Billy Ray Smith of the Colts, and I'm pretty sure he did it every week. Ron does that. You can hear him in the bathroom throwing up when the coach is talking to us and trying to get us ready to play. Well, he had to take a lot of guff from Joe Madro. Like: 'Lou, you make one more bad snap and I'll take your rice away from you.' He called him Mao, or Chou En-lai, and he was always threatening that a rickshaw would arrive to bear Lou away from camp. If Lou got a little too vigorous or desperate on the field during practice—he was a very intense, furious player—Joe would remind him, 'Listen, this is not the cultural revolution, Lou. It's just a football field.' "

"I don't see how he stood it," I said.

"We had a kid who eventually did walk out," Curry said. "Joe Wheelis. He was from Rice Institute in Houston. Madro would mimic his Southwestern accent, and then in reference to what he considered Wheelis's lack of speed, he would ask him, 'Are you really?'

"Wheelis would ask, bewildered, 'Am I really *what?*'

" 'Are you really wheelless? Do you have no wheels? The way you run, you look as if you have no wheels. Your name is very appropriate.'

"I don't think he was truly conscious that this sort of thing could hurt people. He wasn't a bad man at all; he had a bright football mind. He developed a super offensive line at San Diego. But he certainly barraged us with that act of his. He was constantly unloading pithy little asides, and then he'd look at us for reactions. The first time he drew up a basic trap play on the board he made the remark, "Gentlemen, the guy who designed this play lost his Diners Club card at the Last Supper." Then he turned around to check the response. A center would make a high snap and he'd call out, 'Let's get the helium out of that ball.' Always the same. Maybe four or five times a day, we'd hear that shout drifting across the field.

"Or if a halfback dropped a pass, Joe would ask him if a thumb

76

had grown in his palm just before the ball got there. Or to someone who'd made a bad mistake, Joe would say, 'Listen here, Smith. It's my way or Trailways . . .' a reference to the bus company which would be the player's mode of departure if he didn't improve.

"He had these special terms. Anyone who wasn't a big player was a 'lady.' 'What we're trying to do on this play is to get a lady blocking on a lady,' he'd tell us, which meant that a halfback would try to block on a lighter safety or cornerback rather than a big lineman. It makes sense, but you can imagine how the halfbacks liked being referred to as 'ladies.'

"Sometimes he got confused with his own conceits. Once he was talking about the other team lining up in a gap defense, which usually happens in a short yardage or a goal-line situation in which the other team tries to shoot players between us when the ball is snapped. Joe's little phrase was: 'Guard that gap like a virgin mother.' He thought about what he had said, and tried again, 'I mean a mother . . . a daughter . . . I mean the way a virgin . . . the way a mother guards her virgin daughter.'

"If he got lost like this, or made a mistake on the blackboard, he'd look at us and come out with: 'Now I'm floundering on the sea of rudderless destiny.'

"Very often he'd wrap up a meeting by trying to talk to us in modern lingo. One day he said, 'All right now, men, this is important. I want you to understand this. Do you read my vibes? Some linemen get callused ears from listening to me. Okay. Get your asses in gear and do whatever you want.'

"So we'd close our playbooks, and on the way down to practice we'd try to figure out what he meant.

"All this time Sid Gillman was in the wings. He had a heart condition and he wasn't supposed to coach . . . but he could see what was going on. He'd try to assume a little authority. He'd go to Pete: 'Pete, how about if I coach the tight ends.' Pete would refuse. He'd come and tell me that he'd kept Gillman out of the picture. 'That guy's trying to infiltrate.'

"It was depressing to be on the field with someone always looking over his shoulder, and yet hoping for respect and friendship from the players. Paranoia was everywhere. Madro thought the other coaches were stealing things from him—projector lenses, chalk, erasers. He would call us around him and he'd say, 'Now, if an alien comes in here, we can't do it by letting the lady try to pick up the defensive tackle . . . but these dummies over there'—he was referring to the other coaches!—'think we can do it their way. They think the back can step up and meet that guy. Well, lemme tell you something: When I was in San Diego we did it the other way, and that's the way it ought to be done! The old man knows that. I wish they'd let me do my things right. We'd do something! I *guarantee* you, we would improve.' And he would start off on a tirade.

"And so, here the Oilers were. We were expected to go out and line up as a unit and run plays, and yet we had coaches that for all practical purposes were actually competing against each other. I used to imagine one coach with his squad lining up at the north end of the end zone, another at the south end zone, two others with their people on the west side line, two more on the east side . . . and then a whistle would go off and they'd all run plays at each other and end up in a big heap in the middle of the field. That's almost the state we found ourselves in in training camp.

"All this confusion. Joe Madro'd dig into his motivational material: 'It's *now* time. Not tomorrow or yesterday. But now time. *Now* time.'

"And then I'd go to him after the meeting and I'd say, 'Coach, what time is practice this afternoon?'

"He'd say, 'I don't know. I don't know if there's a practice or not.' "

"How did the players survive all this?" I asked.

"As usual, all of this was tempered by humor. That was the only way we could survive. Paul Robinson, one of the halfbacks, was one of those exuberant people who turn up and help make life bearable. He was always laughing and carrying on. Very merry man. His favorite thing that first year was that anybody running in an open field and falling for no good reason had been tackled by these tiny little men down there in the grass. 'You got to watch out for those little men,' he'd say. 'They'll get you, boy. They'll get your foot every *time.* You got to stay out of the tall grass.' He said this in a high little weak voice, which made it funnier.

"One day Paul decided he was going into a business project with his little men. He came to me. He called me Cap, because I was the team captain. 'Hey, Cap, what's happenin', man? What it is? Listen, I got an idea. You know those little mens out there grabbing everybody's feet, making 'em fall down and everything? I'm gonna start a business and have some "little men" insurance. You can get insurance from me so that if'n those little men make you fall down, you can get paid off.'

"He was always talking about how these little men were hiding around behind the stems of the tall grass. I never thought to ask him why people fell down on artificial turf.

"You can imagine what sort of a relief Robinson was in that Houston situation. As for myself, I had this strange dichotomy going on—this contradiction of feelings: enjoying this new-found power of being captain and having an obvious amount of responsibility and at the same time struggling under a pressure that made me feel as if I were walking in mud above my knees. During training camp, I had a recurring dream that I was sitting in the twenty-third-story window of a building. In fact, I was sitting out on the sill! Somebody working with a shovel, of all things, dropped it, and I watched it fall twenty-three stories, bounding back and forth as it hit one wall and then the other, and then shattering at the bottom. In the dream there was a most awesome compulsion for me to follow the shovel, so real that it was terrifying . . . as if somebody had his hand in the small of my back and was trying to boost me on out the window. I kept fighting to fall back into the room, and I always woke up before I found out which way I was going to go. Perhaps my subconscious was telling me to get on out of Houston before everything got worse.

"There *was* a lot of pressure on me. Somehow the people in Houston felt that I was going to walk in from the Baltimore Colts, a halo glowing over my head, and with one hand aloft I was going to part the Red Sea and lead the tribe out of the chains of bondage. When we began to lose—which was immediately, of course—I began to get the feeling that they were looking askance at me as if: Well, we brought this—whatever it was they thought I was—here and he's not doing it. The Houston press had not done anything to help. They had raved on about me . . . about 'all-pro status' and 'ability to articulate.' The pressure was *heavy*. I began to remember this terrible dream I used to have as a child, a nightmare that I have awakened in a strange place—a home not dissimilar from my own—but when I'd get up out of bed and go to the kitchen, there'd be a strange lady there who was not my mother and a man that I didn't know and other people just staring at me as if I had suddenly dropped out of a spaceship . . . an alien in their midst. The dream would always end at that point. It never went far enough for me to know what happened . . . if I was accepted. But it was always so cold and so strange. And that's just exactly how I felt at Houston, except that these strangers were looking at me as a special person with some great power of leadership and ability to change things. And it wasn't working."

"I saw that team play," I said. "You came to New York to play the Giants. I took my English roommate from Cambridge University to the Yankee Stadium to watch you. He'd never seen a football game before."

"I remember," Curry said with a laugh. "You brought him down to the locker room afterward. He looked worried. What a way to introduce someone to the game of football."

I had never had much luck taking the English to football games. I told Curry that years before I had taken an English girl to a Harvard-Brown game at Cambridge, Massachusetts. She had sat staring out at the two teams, playing in the mud. For reasons I've forgotten, I assumed that she knew something about the game. But apparently not, because after ten minutes or so, she turned to me and said that she thought she'd figured it out: What one team was trying to do was to snatch the ball away from the other. Wasn't that it? Well, I said that while I had never quite thought of it that way, come to think of it, her description wasn't a bad one at all. She then asked this piercing question: "Why don't they bring out a ball and give it to the team which doesn't have one? Wouldn't it solve everything?"

Curry laughed. "Well, what did you tell her?"

"I couldn't think of anything to say," I said. "I haven't been able to look at a football game with any sense of equanimity since then."

"I can see why," he said. "I wish you hadn't told *me*. . . . What town are we going by?" He looked up at one of the overhang signs. "Wolcott, Indiana. The place where Bill Curry suddenly became utterly aware of the lunatic aspects of football." He pushed back from the steering wheel and sighed. "Boy, I remember that Giants game. I really thought we were going to play extremely well. We'd had great practices. The Giants were one of the worst teams in the NFL, though at the time they were riding the crest, 6 and 0 in exhibition. But I considered them very ripe. I thought we were going to kill them. We had this great quarterback, very good receivers, super running backs, a few frogs in the offensive line, and problems with our linebackers, but I thought it'd be a high-scoring game and we'd win. We had a great chapel service that morning. The speaker was excellent. Just excellent! He was a black guy, an associate of a fellow named Tom Skinner, who is the chaplain for the Redskins and grew up in the inner city and once was a gang leader in New York. This guy said some meaningful things that day about a community of action—this very thing that I feel so strongly about: how groups of people come together to accom-

81

plish things. He was just superb. Fred Willis, sitting next to me, was deeply moved by what he said. He was a quiet kind of guy, but a phenomenal athlete, and the sort of potential leader that the Oilers were looking for. We discussed the talk and how good it was. After our pregame meal we went on out to the stadium. The tension was building, and the team was ready. I just *knew* they were ready. I've never felt so strongly that we were going to play well. Then Fred stood up and said, "I don't usually say much, but we had a chapel speaker this morning that was just dynamite; I want to share with you a little bit of what he had to say.' Then there was a long pause. 'Damn, I can't remember. Curry, what'd he say?' I swear he did that! So then I had to stand up and say, 'Well, fellows, what he said was . . .'

"It was typical of the day. We went right out on the field and threw an interception and they scored a touchdown against us; another interception: touchdown . . . and before we knew it, it was 27 to nothing. Freddy and I stood on the sidelines. We were playing hard and just getting killed. He said, 'I can't believe any of this.' I said, 'I can't either.'

"That game was typical of the whole season. The self-doubt and the pressure began to tell. Later on, we played a game against Pittsburgh, which had a vastly superior team, but we had the lead 7 to 6 at the half. We were playing extremely well and I fully expected to beat them. In the second half we came out and Pastorini threw a few interceptions and then we began to make mistakes; we fell apart and they just annihilated us. They kept laying it on me. I was the new president of the Players Association—John Mackey had just retired, which automatically moved me up—and they had a lot of fun with that. Tom Keating came in the game for the Steelers and I heard him say 'El Presidente!' just pointing up the embarrassment of my situation. I was able to cut him. That was the only enjoyable thing about the day. They kept expecting us to pass, but we were so far out of the game that we were running the ball to get it over with and I was able to knock Keating down five or six times. I laughed at him and beat on his sore knee with my fist at the bottom of the pileup. Then I lost my temper. I got kicked in the face by their middle linebacker and I tried to knock him down. There was Keating in front of me again, laughing and saying, 'Mr. President, Mr. President. Please, you're embarrassing us.'

"Then my good friend Andy Russell, who had played a phenomenal game on the field, came up afterward and began to commiserate with me. Andy had been through about eight years of Steeler teams, which had a reputation for being just about the worst in the history of the game. In fact, back with the Colts, Alex Hawkins' imitation of a Steeler sitting on the bench with his head down between his legs is one of the funniest routines I've ever seen. But they were on top now, and Andy came over and began to jest about the fact that you never could really trust somebody unless he had been on a losing team. I didn't know much about being on a losing team. I began to choke up; he began to stammer and really didn't know what to say except, 'Gee, Bill, I'm . . . you know, I . . . uh . . . I didn't mean to . . . I wasn't trying to be, uh, sarcastic or anything. You know, I . . .'

"I think around that time if I had met that English girl of yours and she'd asked me that question about why not bring out another ball, I'd have thrown in the towel . . . just happily walked out of football and forgotten it."

Chapter 8

Near Remington, Indiana, we stopped and I took over the driving. Once again Curry took the opportunity to exercise his leg. He trotted a hundred yards up the highway, and then back. When we got going, he began telling me about his injury. It had been the first serious one of his career. In a game against the Los Angeles Rams, he was dropping back on pass protection and got hit unexpectedly from his left side behind his knee, and then a blow came down on the tibial plateau—which is where the front part of the leg comes up to the knee—knocking off a portion of it and impacting it into the tibia. On the operating table the bone was replaced with a piece from the hospital's bone bank, a pin was placed completely through the knee, and the torn medial collateral ligaments were patched up . . . some very extensive surgery, and he had quite a bit of time to reflect on exactly what had happened, and what it was going to mean to him.

Curry began to reminisce about it. "The old adage runs that

you don't have a single friend on a football field," he said. "It's true. The NFL field is alive with hostility. Some players feign it, others are quite natural about it, and others—which is my attitude—try to ignore it and do their jobs. I don't like the hostile attitude—the notion that you're supposed to hate your opponent. Certainly it's there when you play—an almost palpable force.

But when I was hurt I went from no friends to twenty-one in a split second. My injury was very obvious. I lay there screaming. I've never seen anybody behave like that on the field—but it was an instant and awesome, terrifying pain. When the initial edge of the pain began to withdraw, the first thing I sensed was human concern. It enveloped me . . . the Rams and the other players leaning over; Youngblood, I think it was, of the Rams shouting for the trainers and the doctors to hurry up. I remember Fred Dryer and Merlin Olsen, and of course Dan Pastorini of our own team . . . and Billy Parks's face, which was pure anguish, and when I was carried alongside our bench on a stretcher, Ron Mayo, one of our rookies, kept putting a cold towel on my face, and I could feel a hand touch my shoulder, or tousle my hair, just a succession of these hands reaching out as I went along the bench . . . and it was a tremendous sensation, almost a heady feeling.

"When I got to the hospital, almost immediately they gave me a sedative, which got me calmed down, but also tended to loosen my tongue at both ends. Sid Gillman came, one of the first to see me; I asked him how long the situation was going to go on. Sid didn't blink. He said, 'Well, we're handling this the best way we can.'

"People began to call. Howard Cosell. He seemed tired on the phone, and I asked him about his health. He said he had been going very hard. He was going to finish broadcasting the football season and then he was going to review his whole life. I'm not exactly sure what he meant by that. He said he had been making the rounds of the Hollywood shows—Sonny and Cher,

Dean Martin, and things like that. I asked him if he enjoyed that sort of thing. He said, 'Yes, I do. One simply has to get away from the sports thing sometimes. It can *consume* you.' It sounded kind of familiar. He said, 'Don't people know there's a goddam war in the Mideast! Baseball people, they think of baseball. They can think of *nothing* else. You must realize,' he said, 'we're dealing with dugout mentalities here.' It was nice of him to call. I remember some players were sitting around with him once and Jim Houston asked him which was the most fascinating interview he had done, and Howard said without any hesitation, 'With myself!'

"Other people called. A guy named Bruce Randall . . . very bright guy . . . has the world's largest collection of Tiffany lamps and owns an estate out in Long Island near New York City. He called me in the hospital and he said, 'I just want to say one thing to you and I want you to think about it.'

" 'Okay, fine.'

" 'Just remember this statement: "The dust from whence we come." '

"I repeated it. ' "The dust from whence we come"?'

" 'Yup,' he said. ' "The dust from whence we come," and that's all I have to say. Just remember that now and we'll talk about it someday.'

" 'Gee, fine,' I said. 'Okay.'

"I haven't talked to him since. Terrific guy. I can hardly wait to find out what he meant by it. Any ideas?"

"I'm afraid I can't help you," I said.

"Well, whatever, I had a lot to think about," Curry said. "I kept thinking back about the game, on the injury, and I kept trying to remember how I was prior to the injury and what its effect had been on me. The Ram game had been hard, fast-paced. . . . a lot of movement, a lot of intensity. More so than usual. Merlin Olsen, I remember, was just coming and coming with his great strength, not quite as fast as he used to be, but strong and *intense*. His greatness really doesn't stem from size and speed, or even intelligence; it's a burning, simmering ability to focus, to intensify. It's almost like a magnifying glass and a pile of leaves. It smolders; it threatens to burst into flame all the time. You know it's there; you hold him at bay; you struggle; you scrap; you dig into your guts to summon your own intensity, fighting the feeling of intimidation that comes from a person like this, who never, ever, lets up. And fighting an almost certain knowledge that sooner or later he *is* going to flame up . . . his intensity is going to overpower yours at some point, perhaps at a crucial point and you'll be defeated. All through the game I was fighting that familiar grim battle with Merlin Olsen. Surprisingly, one rather enjoys the challenge of that sort of thing . . . always, of course, with the expectation of overcoming the other player, of having one's *own* intensity outshine his or burst into flame more brightly or more quickly. . . .

"So I lost the battle. Not that Merlin would have ever injured me intentionally. But his fire overpowered mine. Or, as chance would have it, my flame was snuffed out."

"What about fear?" I asked.

"Fear. Of course," Curry said, "I was afraid there was something badly wrong with my knee, even though I kept trying to tell myself it was only just a massive bruise. But then I also had the fear that I would be embarrassed . . . that after having been taken out on a stretcher into an ambulance, they would find that there was nothing wrong with my leg. So there was almost a fear that I was *not* hurt . . . and I rather hoped I was, at least enough to justify all the hullabaloo that attended my leaving the Astrodome.

"Then the fear of the operation . . . remembering a player named Mack Lee Hill, who had played for the Kansas City Chiefs in 1965. I became very frightened. Mack Lee Hill experienced a knee injury, went in for a rather routine knee operation, was placed under general anesthesia, and just never woke up. He died on the operating table, because of the anesthetic itself, or some reaction he had. When the anesthetist came in to me, this great fear began to grow that somehow there would be a mistake made. It was intensified because I'd been through quite an upheaval in my personal faith . . . a radical change from a very conservative, almost fundamental Christian viewpoint to a near-agnostic view. When I found myself reduced to fearing for my life—whether or not it was rational—I involved myself fervently in prayer. Once again I understood the mentality of the fundamental Christian who most of all fears dying and somehow missing his reward. All that inculcation through my upbringing, my early years, came back and I began to apologize to God for having doubted and having been overly, perhaps, intellectual in the pursuit of my faith; I went on to apologize for not communicating with regularity, and especially for calling on Him at this point. But I explained that I was in trouble, that I was afraid, that I needed Him to watch over me, and that very much I wanted Him to understand that at this moment of stress I did in fact return to a genuine belief.

"In fact, I think all this goes right to the heart of this matter of football being a practical religion in this country . . . with its origins in the 'fear' that consumes both the players and the people watching. When I talk about fear, I'm talking about the fear of failure, the fear of missing one's final reward, and wanting a justification for one's existence—all of which can be solved by victory. Victory. Nothing else. It happens every Sunday across this land. People with fanatical feelings toward a group of men whom they admire very much and to whom they pay great tribute every week with their roars and their screaming and their waving of handkerchiefs. They're exorcising this fear in themselves, achieving a sort of catharsis . . . literally using the game of football as a religion, as a cleansing experience, as a solace. The question that arises is whether or not it is, in fact, healthy. The violent aspect is obviously unhealthy for men who shatter their knees. As for its impact on society, I don't know now. I used to feel that it *was* a great cleansing thing. But then

I just didn't know, and I'm not sure I know now."

"You must have had an odd reaction seeing your first game after that experience," I said.

"Very strange. They wheeled me out to the Astrodome up to an area known as the Skybox. It's set aside for people who can afford very expensive, exclusive areas of their own . . . with butlers, and catered food, and closed-circuit television so they can watch the game even if they choose not to sit in their allotted seats. I was full of pain pills to keep my leg from bothering me, and I was a little delirious. I took a rather dim view of the proceedings. It was all rather nightmarish in quality. The players and the playing surface and the bands and the majorettes, all the trappings that are part of the game, seemed foolish and less than real—out of proportion and very much like a dream—as if I were looking down into some fantasy land where people were attempting to create an art form and failing miserably at it. I couldn't get into the whole thing. I made a few feeble attempts at cheering and getting excited. Maybe I would have felt better had the team played better. They showed some signs of life in the first half, but in the second half they came out and, in just a total display of ineptitude, were bombed by the Denver Broncos, not the greatest team in the world themselves. The final score was 48 to 20. It was really just the most depressing day. I was actually relieved to get back to the hospital.

"In fact, I tried to convince myself for seven months that I didn't want to play anymore. One of my first memories after coming out from the anesthesia and all the drugs after the operation on my leg was a Monday-night football game. Washington and Dallas were playing; it was October 8, just about twenty-four hours after I had been operated on. I remember thinking: Boy, I'm glad I don't ever have to do that again! Look at those fools! Every time I saw a hit on a guy I'd wince. Of course, my leg was killing me. There's not enough morphine—unless they knock you out completely—to keep it from hurting.

The very thought of going out and having it hit again was horrifying . . . it would just bring me off the bed, almost! I'd think: What have I been doing all my life? This is insanity!

"So it started with that. But after a while it slowly became a conflict. I'd begin thinking: It's getting time now to start putting myself in shape; my knee will take it. Dan Pastorini walked in my room right after the operation and leaned over and said, 'Don't think for one second that just because you bumped your leg that you're going to leave me out there on the field to rot by myself! You're not getting out of this.' Every time I talked about hanging it up, he just smiled: 'You'll be back. You'll be back for one reason.'

" 'What's that?' I'd ask.

" 'Me. I'm going to kill you if you don't.'

"Pastorini loved the game so much he'd get choked up talking about it. He used to say that if you didn't get excited about what you enjoyed, you were only half a person. He wondered how the end of his football career could ever come with his wanting to quit. He couldn't imagine himself saying, 'I no longer want to play.' Perhaps: 'I *can* no longer play,' but never: 'I no longer *want* to play.'

"Other players turned up. I remember a delightful visit from a fellow named Tom Regner. Strangely enough, he was the player the Oilers traded to the Baltimore Colts for me the January before—Tom Regner and a third-round draft choice, for me. One day when we first got back to Houston from training camp, Ron Saul asked me if I'd like to join him over a sandwich and we went to a place called the Venetian Village, which was within walking distance of the practice field. There behind the bar making sandwiches stood Tom Regner. I had heard that he had planned on retiring, but I had no idea what he was doing. He was in the restaurant business, so I had the unique experience of having my lunch prepared each day by the player who was traded for me.

"Well, Tom had gone through some football operations, and

he knew about hospital food; so he used to bring me a couple of what they call 'poor boy' sandwiches. We had great visits. We laughed about his brief time in Baltimore when he went to one of Coach Schnellenberger's camps and was forced to run around the field a certain number of times and couldn't do it. He's called Pear because of the shape of his body. He had a considerable degree of difficulty negotiating this six-lap run and he had been scolded and kicked by the coaches. That day he made his decision that he would give up this foolishness. We agreed that he had left at the right time; he finished after having played six years in the NFL.

"He was a great storyteller. We started talking about some of the crazy things that happen, some of the really wacky things. He told me about a quarterback he used to play with, named Pete Beathard, who afterward played with Kansas City. Beathard used to get so nervous trying to call a play that he would throw up in the huddle. . . . Tom's mimicry of Beathard was just great. He'd start calling his play, and then he'd begin to gag little by little, until he was literally vomiting the play from his mouth. Then up at the line of scrimmage, Tom, playing guard next to the center, Bobby Maples, said that he could hear Beathard trying to call out the cadence and continuing to lose his pregame meal on the back of Bobby Maples' jersey. I mean, I was always a little nervous before a game, but my gosh, I've never heard of anything like that.

"It reminded me of the time in Dallas when Cornelius Johnson, who was the guard for us on the Colts at that time, got a little overheated and threw up on Bob Lilly's hands. Lilly jumped up and hollered, you know, and drew his hands back. Just about that time we snapped the ball, went ahead, and ran the play, and Bob had the unfortunate distinction of being the only person standing up at the time. A year later when we went back to play Dallas, we came up over the ball, and Corny faked his illness this time, kind of belching a couple of times like he was gonna throw up, and Lilly jumped back and stood up again, apparently remembering what had happened the previous year."

I asked, "Did any of the players advise you not to go on?"

"Billy Ray Smith did," Curry replied. "The Rabbit. He tore his leg all to pieces early in his career. He's really a wonderful weird old dog who grew up in the backwoods in Arkansas, acts backwoods, and *is* backwoods—he wears cowboy hats and boots —the most unrefined person you'll ever meet, yet a buffoon with a mind like a steel trap. We established a rapport early when I was with the Colts; he took me under his wing. Wonderful old character. He tried to teach me lessons about life. He was concerned that I was too naïve, and he wanted me to understand that everybody was going to stick it to me sooner or later. That had been his experience in his life. I told him there were some decent folks. He said if that was true, he hadn't run across many of them.

"In our hospital talks, he was very adamant about my not playing anymore. He said, 'For gosh sakes, don't be playing this stupid stuff. Look what I did to myself.' His body really is a wreck. He was a big, powerful, awesome tough guy, and still is, but he's gnarled and broken.

"But then, you see, there were the others. Ordell Braase, the great defensive end who had played twelve or thirteen years with the Colts, took me aside and said, 'I don't know how bad that leg is. But whatever you do, whatever you have to go through, do it and play football.' He was very solemn about it. He said, 'Boy, after you've had the experience of pro football, *nothing* else is satisfying! It is so *dull* in the business world.' It happens that he is doing phenomenally well—a restaurant business and a couple of other things. But he said it was just so *boring* . . . that no matter what I had to do, I should get myself ready and play. Another one was John Matuszak. He kept badgering me. John has the most staggering physical dimensions that I've ever seen . . . 290, trim, perfect physique, six foot eight, and he wears elevator heels which lift him up to about seven feet! When he walks down the street people are just agog. You can't imagine him. And he can fly! He can run. He's got all this potential. He's going to be a very good player. And *he* started in on me. But when I looked at him I wondered why in the world . . . *why?* He is exactly the guy that I would have to practice against every day, and here he was, this enormous specimen I'd have to compete against. 'You've got to play. You've got to play.' "

"Why do you suppose they were so adamant?" I asked. "I mean, apart from wanting you back on the Oilers?"

"Because it *is* a great wrench," Curry said. "I always knew that if I quit, my relationship with those friends would be different. Football is a very exclusive fraternity. Once you walk away from it, you're just not included anymore; you're out of the deal. Every retired player I've talked to, without exception, has said, when I asked if he missed it: 'No, I don't miss it at all. Who wants to go out there and sweat?' Then they get a funny look on their face and they say, 'But I tell you what, I miss the guys.' It's always the same thing . . . 'the guys' or 'the fellows.' "

"Did you talk to Carolyn about it?" I asked.

"Carolyn and I talked about it an awful lot. So much of our well-being and our relationship is based on my being involved in something that I'm happy with. That's what she wants, from both the unselfish and the selfish standpoints. She didn't want me to go back if I was going to detest it. Nor did she want me to quit if I was going to be miserable.

"I kept wondering what Lombardi would have advised. He'd probably have said, 'If you decide not to play, don't do it because of some manufactured reason . . . that you've got a little fracture of your leg. That's something you can overcome. If *that's* the reason you're quitting, you're copping out. If you're quitting, on the other hand, because you feel like you've played all you should, that you've made your contribution, and that now you're going to step out and move on to the next plateau, then quit.' That's what I think he'd say. Which didn't help things at all."

"Well, how on earth *did* you decide?"

"I guess I knew what my decision was going to be when I checked my reaction at the last Houston game of the year. What a difference from those games I saw when I was first injured. The game was against Cincinnati. I was down to the sideline on crutches and I got completely involved emotionally. I was going to sit on the bench and watch, but the Oilers were playing such fan*tas*tic football that I got right next to the field; I could've had the other leg broken. Pastorini was 21 out of 25 throwing the football. Freddy Willis was running all over the field. Then that incredible rookie Isaac Curtis of the Bengals caught two long bombs and won the game for Cincinnati. But they were just defeated in every other way. I was up screaming on the sidelines. A fight broke out on the field. It was Al Jenkins, who was number 60, though it wasn't his fault. The referee came running over and said, 'Number 50 is out of the game.' Number 50! That was *my* number. He'd got it wrong. I was so emotionally involved that I poled my way out onto the field on my crutches, rushing up, pushing guys out of the way, and I shouted, 'I'm number 50, I'm number 50! You see me?' The poor ref had the funniest look on his face. I mean, to look up and see this crazed man out on the field on crutches. Then Gillman came over and said, 'We don't even have a 50, you stupid ass!' They kicked Al Jenkins out anyhow.

"So even on crutches, I knew I'd come around. I had to play football again."

Chapter 9

The one subject on our trip north that seemed to spook Curry
—he talked about his injury freely enough—was his involve-
ment with the Players Association. When his teammate John
Mackey retired from the presidency of the organization in the
fall of 1973, Curry succeeded him. It was a very difficult time.
Not only was he being forced by his injury to wonder about his
future in active football, but extremely volatile issues were at
stake in the showdown between the players and the owners.
People yelled at him in the street, he told me. Negotiations had
been broken off. The strike was ineffectual . . . and the players
began to drift back to the clubs. Nothing had been resolved—
which made all that expenditure of time and effort seem so
fruitless.

We had talked about the question in the past—Curry had
always been very loquacious and proud of what he was doing.
But now, when I brought up the question, he turned up the
radio slightly and we listened to the music as we drove along,

and we talked about other things, idly, until finally, almost as if he had been storing up what he wanted to say, he clicked off the radio and began talking about why he was so discouraged.

"The single greatest barrier," he said, "is a serious lack of understanding of what a modern professional athlete is like. Some coaches—and they're supposed to be close to the players —still insist on having a guy get his hair cut a certain length . . . not just to look neat or clean, but to have it a certain length so that it can't protrude out from under a headgear more than x number of inches . . . it shouldn't flow in the wind or something. Now, that's not a big deal. Most guys really don't care that much about cutting their hair. But there's something symbolic about a grown man being told how he should dress and how he must wear his hair. That sort of thing.

"The insulation between players and owners is even thicker. As in most cases, it's not fair to generalize, but the owners do seem to share a reasonably common problem: they don't really believe that the players are serious about such matters; they really feel that it's such a privilege for a young man to come into the NFL that he shouldn't be concerned with the kinds of principles we've just been talking about. He shouldn't be too concerned about what kind of surface he plays on. Some stadium authority is purported to have said during the artificial-turf dispute: 'Well, they'll play on asphalt if you pay 'em enough.'

"Somehow the situation must evolve where owners can sit down with players and talk about the problems without being insulted by the fact that they have to be in a room with us."

"What *was* it like in there?" I asked.

"Well, at the meetings there's always friendliness at first . . . but only as long as we don't start reaching over and touching the sacred cow, or wandering into the old Indian burial grounds. You get in those areas, buddy, and you've got a hot Indian on your hands. You can't talk to them about whether or not it makes sense to till that soil; it's just sacred ground. Just don't tread on that! And once you do, brother, the *whole* atmosphere changes. It drives them to do very disturbing things.

"We didn't understand how ironclad they were in their traditions. How could we expect that Wellington Mara, the owner of the Giants, could talk about diminishing the power of the commissioner? If you did a little homework into his character and his feelings about the league, you would understand that to him it's like the *church*. It's *that* sacred.

"So when you're dealing with people like Mara, you have to be very firm, but also politic. We started out that first meeting in 1974 in gentlemanly enough fashion. I opened by saying that the mark of a successful football team was mutual respect and trust. I said that I hoped the two groups sitting at the table would also create such an atmosphere . . . that we had mutual interests, and that thus we could go forward in the negotiations in an expeditious manner. Wellington Mara was very gracious. He said, 'I wish I could've used those words myself.'

"But then Ed Garvey, our executive director, read a statement—which we had all seen—in which, in very frank and strident language we told the owners that we were well aware of the things that they'd done to us in the negotiations back in 1970—threatening, fining, and cutting people for participating in collective action—and that this time we expected them to behave like gentlemen. Well, it just blew their minds. Infuriated them! It was stupid of us. They were so upset that they really weren't ever going to talk to us.

"Their reaction seemed to be reflected by the public. It was very hard to get our side of the story out . . . especially when you're competing against twenty-six PR offices around the league representing each team. In 1970, for example, the owners took our pension proposals, and using some still unexplained actuarial methods, came up with the report that we were demanding a pension for a fifteen-year veteran that at the age of sixty-five would amount to $65,000 a year! It wasn't true. But that would get out to the press through this huge disseminating apparatus of theirs and the public would go crazy with indignation that we would be asking for such ludicrous things.

"It's true that we went way overboard in our initial proposals: we had too many of them—ninety-three. That was out of naïveté. We numbered them, and that was even more stupid. They were called demands because that is a common labor term: We demand. The NFL Players Association was in no position to 'demand.' That's just semantics. We could've had *one* demand; we could have had seven. The only reason we put a number alongside was for convenience . . . like when the preacher stands up and says, 'We're going to sing hymn number 58,' everybody knows where to turn! Well, that's the only reason we did that. But it was a terrible mistake. Because it was very natural for the public to exclaim, "Ninety-three!" They thought to themselves: Well, the last time the laborers negotiated down in Atlanta, they had *three* demands. And look at these jerk football players who're making $100,000 apiece—that's what a lot of people think—and they've got *ninety-three* things they want! So it just wasn't very smart. We came off arrogant. We're going to do this, and we're going to do that. And we didn't get it done. And still haven't gotten it done. We worked very hard to condense these things and to do it right, and *thought* we were doing it right, but we were a bunch of youngsters in this business and we didn't!

"Lord, there could have been three thousand demands. One of them, I remember, was based on the possibility of compulsory urinalysis for football players to test for drugs. Like race horses. Pee-in-the-bucket kind of thing. One of the owners, in his wisdom, made the analogy: 'I don't see anything wrong with urinalysis. To me, it's kind of like going on an airplane and having my bags go through a detector." One of the counter-suggestions made by a player was that before each session of Congress each congressman pee in a bottle and before each meeting of the Supreme Court all the justices submit to urinalysis. He was furious. Why us? Mike Stratton made a fascinating proposal. Just a delightful guy! He played for Buffalo for many years, a great linebacker. He thought that it would be a good idea if we had a pregame ceremony in which each team would line up down the sidelines. Just after the National Anthem, everyone would face toward the inside of the field. Whereupon a long piece of litmus paper would be stretched the length of the team. Each man in turn would step forward and pee on the litmus paper. The crowd could go up in a mighty roar if it was the right color; it meant the player was going to get to play that day. If, on the other hand, he didn't make it because there was something wrong with his urine, then there'd be a groan and everybody'd watch him retire to the dressing room. I thought that was a great idea! But we didn't put it in; we thought it was a little radical."

I asked if the owners had given in on any of the demands.

"The owners capitulated on very few," Curry said. "One was that there'd be no more personality testing of the veterans. These were tests in which a player was shown Rorschach blots and asked about his mom and so forth, and then his coach was supposed to interpret whether the player was psychologically fit . . . whether he had killer instincts, that sort of thing. The results went into a player's file and they could be disseminated, and indeed were, to prospective employers after a player left football, and in a couple of cases even to the press. It leaked out that two or three players were hopelessly psychotic, according to these tests, and the first they knew about it was when they read it in the newspaper. Incredible.

"Well, the owners conceded on that one. Two or three more. They also agreed to form subcommittees to discuss the subject of subcommittees."

"Terrific," I said.

"So it went," Curry continued. "Our intent was never to destroy or disrupt the game of football. Those of us who've thought about it really believe that some compromises, some changes in the system to allow for *some* mobility by players, to allow for a sensible system of appeal of grievances and problems that arise, would not destroy the league at all; it would solve a lot of problems.

"One of the main problems is Commissioner Rozelle's being an "impartial arbitrator." He can't be. He's paid by the owners. We got in an argument one day, and one of the owners slammed his hand down on the table, jumped up, and said, 'Dammit, don't be telling us Rozelle's not neutral. We pay him damn well to be neutral.' It's wrong. Why should he be saddled with that question: Are you really neutral? What do you think the National Academy of Arbitrators' position would be if one of their members was paid a quarter of a million dollars a year by General Motors and sat there ruling on the UAW–General Motors disputes and tried to say he was neutral? I mean, really!

"The owners' answer always is: 'Well, we're not General Motors and you're not the UAW. This business is unique; this is *football.*' Well, perhaps football *is* different, and maybe it's even unique, but we're still people with families; we're black guys who don't want to go to one place or another, and white guys that don't want to go somewhere because they're uncomfortable . . . and it's hard to see why it would destroy the game for them to have, at some point in their career, the opportunity to go where they want to live and where they want to start building their lives for the next fifty years.

"Well, the argument goes, 'If you work for IBM, they move you all over the country, and you have no choice.' The fact is you damn sure do have a choice! If you don't like it there, you can go over to Xerox; if you're good at what you do, you can always ply your trade. But if you're a good football player for the National Football League, you're stuck. If you want to move, the Rozelle Rule applies—where you play out the option and the team to which you move must offer proper compensation to the team you leave. A sportscaster asked me about the Rozelle Rule the other day. 'Really, what is this thing? What's the problem? I really don't understand.' I said, 'Okay, let's take your situation with NBC here in Washington. You want to go over to NBC in Minneapolis. Your grandmother lives there or something. But before you could go, you'd have to *stay* in Washington a year playing out your option, forgo any raise (suppose you were Sportscaster of the Year and had a good raise coming), plus take a 10 percent pay cut just for the privilege of negotiating with the Minneapolis people. And then, before you can go, the two stations have to arrive at a compensation determined by someone paid by those two stations, not by AFTRA, not by the people that represent *you*, who will decree that before you can go, Minneapolis has to give up one anchorman and two weather girls to Washington to get you.'

"So what needs to be done?" I asked. "Where do you start?"

"Well, the National Football League constitution and bylaws need to be revised, a revision to go along with the modern moods, the modern feelings. It's as simple as that. Dr. Margaret Mead stood up some years ago in Atlanta at a symposium and said, 'We're about to see little people begin to stand up for themselves all across this country.' I thought about her a hundred times during our struggle because, sure enough, the things that she predicted are coming true. One example: the garbage men in Atlanta struck. Now, instead of forcing them to walk through your yard and pick up your garbage can, you've got to take it down to the street two times a week. That's the way it ought to be. Doesn't matter how rich you are, you've still got to take your garbage to the street. And it saves some tax money. Of course, many people—football people—have made fun of me for using this as an illustration, and while we're certainly not downtrodden little people in terms of collective strength—financially, politically, and otherwise—as opposed to the folks on the other side of the table, we most certainly are. Well, we stood up, and we were thrown back. So we have sought other methods: we've gone to the courts, to the National Labor Relations Board, to the Justice Department, to Congress. . . . Our intent is not to destroy or disrupt the game of football," he

101

emphasized again. "Our allegiance is to the sport that we think is great, which we all, at one time or another, have loved in varying degrees.

"Frankly, I always thought the negotiations were going to work out. True, sometimes we might as well have been talking to the wall. One day I said, 'Mr. Mara, I'm curious about the fact that you revealed the terms of some players' contracts publicly. I've been told for years that's something we don't do—ever talk to each other about the terms of our contracts. My question is: Are you going to continue this? Are we going to see our contracts in the paper? I'm just curious. . . .'"

" 'I agree with you,' he said.

" 'What do you mean?'

" 'I agree that you're curious. . . .'

"But I didn't believe their attitude was going to stay that way. I thought as the pressure mounted, reasonable minds would prevail: 'Hey, listen, this is foolish. Let's get this dadgummed thing solved!'

"I was naïve. I didn't realize that it takes a lot to get fifty-four-year-old ideas changed. It doesn't mean they're evil. Some of them are fine people. But the fact is that you don't change their minds by sitting there and discussing it, or even threatening them with a strike.

"I've often wondered what Lombardi would have done. He was in the '68 negotiations, and quite outspoken, quite an advocate for the owners' position. But at that time we were talking about pension contributions, not about the structure of the game. Frankly, I think that he would've been a pretty strong advocate of the owners' position. But knowing what he said to people like Bart Starr (who stood up strongly for us) when he got back to camp—saying that he would've stuck up for the players, too, if he were playing—you knew that he was talking about an *honorable* fight.

"Right now the players are kind of afraid. They've been browbeaten. Last summer . . . a lot of scary phone calls went over the wires! 'You get to camp! Know what's gonna happen to you? You ain't gonna have a job in football. We've got four rookies in here that look twice as good as you.' So players get nervous; they can see how ugly it can get. A lot of them are saying right now: 'Hey, let's don't rush things . . . let's don't be doing that again! You almost cost me my job last time. You *did* cost four of my buddies their jobs.'

"So the players are not as fierce about the freedom aspects as they were a year ago. But unless the system changes, it won't be long before they'll get their backs up again. I believe that. The owners can get rid of me and the leadership, and *all* of us, but in a year, or two years, or whatever it is down the road, they're going to look across the table and they're going to see the *same mentality* sitting there, saying, 'You've got to change this system. You've *got to* change the system!'"

Chapter 10

At the end of Curry's disquisition on the player-owner problems, I said that I had never understood—considering the travail and the pressures of those negotiations—how he could keep reminding himself that his true function was to *play* the game rather than talk about it. It seemed so incongruous to think of him there in those meeting rooms with the cigarette smoke and the polished tables and the owners looking at him across the sheaves of paper.

Curry winced. "What made it tough," he said, "was that as soon as the hours of negotiation were done, the Oilers, who were in Washington for the meetings, took me on as a project. I only weighed 210; my leg was very weak. We'd rush out of the negotiations to a weight room and Fred Willis would destroy me in there. Then we'd pick up some Gatorade and drink it on the way to the Georgetown University track, where Willis and Pastorini, along with Tom Keating and Kermit Alexander, would run me until I couldn't stand up . . . especially Fred. It was tough! An awful lot of pain.

"Did the fact that you were involved with the negotiations affect your relationship with the Oilers hierarchy?" I asked.

"After the negotiations had broken off, I reported to Huntsville, Texas, where the Oilers had their training camp that year. Sid Gillman called me in and said I wasn't to say anything to the team about the negotiations, or to the press: 'No comment.' He went on to say that he thought the players were going to lose the strike, but that he didn't care one way or the other. 'If you win the strike and we win football games, I'll be happy. If you lose the strike and we win football games, I'll be happy. If Bud Adams'—the owner—'loses money and we win games, I'll be happy. . . .' The kind of stereotype language you get from the old coach image. I'm sure it was honest.

"But when I asked Joe Madro for a playbook and to sit down with him so I'd have some grasp of the offense by the time I started practice, he said he'd like to do that, but he just didn't have time. It was the oddest feeling, having been the captain of the offensive team the year before, with the coaches spending an inordinate amount of time with me, and now suddenly I wasn't worth the time to go over the basic plays with. . . . So I went out and ran several miles every day. I was on the weight program. About three days before the doctors said I'd be ready for contact work, Sid Gillman called me and said, 'I've got three centers here and I don't have time to wait for your leg to heal. We don't need you.'"

"Did they let you go because of your relationship with the Players Association?" I asked.

"I've been very guarded about saying that," Curry said. "But seven players who'd been involved in the strike, a couple of whom had driven all night to get to the training camp at Huntsville, were cut at the first meeting, without even having a chance to practice. Gillman said he couldn't find them, didn't know how to contact them to keep them from coming in—but it's hard for me to understand how an organization could not know its own players' phone numbers, or their addresses.

"Whatever, he let me decide how I wanted it done. I left the room, and after a while I sent back word that I wanted to be put on waivers. I could have retired, but I didn't really want to get out of football; I wanted to give football every opportunity to keep me in."

"It couldn't have been very hard to leave that place," I said.

"No, it was not hard to leave. Several guys came to my room: Al Cowlings, Tody Smith, Fred Hoaglin, Freddy Willis, Dan Pastorini; they helped me pack up, and they carried my stuff to the car. It was like a funeral march; you expected some Bach to thunder suddenly out of the sky. I don't mean that my leaving was *that* big a deal to them; I probably manufactured some of that in my mind. But they are some of my best friends. And we weren't very happy. I tried to say some funny things, and nobody laughed. I distinctly remember them standing on the curb when I drove off in my rental car, and how it was like I was driving off into the sunset. Actually, I thought it was sort of funny . . . a sense of relief and release at being out of that situation.

"When I got back to Atlanta, I really didn't expect any team to pick me up. This was on a Friday morning. A writer called me at home on Saturday morning—from the *Baltimore Sun,* I think—and asked me what my attitude was. I said, 'Well, actually I'm quite busy right now because I've organized the Highlands football team, and you're interrupting my practice.' I was talking about the kids in my own front yard—Kristin Curry, Billy Curry, and Matthew Baughan, Maxie's four-year-old son. I gave their weights and their heights. 'Billy is three foot two, fifty-three pounds. I told him that we had been in the middle of tackling drill when Carolyn had called me to the phone. I started talking about Billy's potential and the fact that he was showing a little progress but really wasn't the kind of hitter I needed for my linebackers; and that Matthew Baughan had great agility but I wondered if he had the killer instinct. . . . I was giving him all the old clichés and having fun.

"With some wonder, the reporter said, 'Well, you've retained your sense of humor in all this.' I said what was obvious: 'I think that's the only link to sanity.'

"Well, then that night the Los Angeles Rams called. First of all, they asked me about my leg and I said it was coming along, it probably would be ready in a couple of weeks. Then they asked how much I weighed. So odd, considering that just a few hours before I'd been giving those tiny weights of the children. I said 235. They said, 'Well, we understood from Houston that you weighed 195.' 'Isn't that interesting,' I replied. Of course, it's tough for somebody to play center at 235, much less 195. 'Well,' I said, 'there's a real easy way to find out if I'm telling the truth or not.'

"So there I was with the Los Angeles Rams, working away at the sport again."

He pointed out the car window. "Hey, there's a game like the one in my front yard." A group of kids were playing in a field. "Well, actually they're a lot bigger. Look at them wearing tear-away jerseys with the big numbers. There isn't one of those kids catching the ball who doesn't imagine that it was tossed to him by a John Unitas or a Bart Starr . . . and that what they're doing out there is getting ready for the big time. They'll drive themselves all those long afternoons to do it—those pudgy kids who don't see very well and lose their specs in the grass. But you know all about that, George," he said, looking over. "You finally got your chance—both the Lions and the Colts."

I stirred somewhat uneasily and said that I had joined those NFL teams in order to write about the experience, more then, well, to play out any childhood fantasy . . . though of course I remembered those long afternoons, too.

"Sure," said Curry, not unkindly.

We drove along for a while, watching the fields sail by. Curry reached forward and turned up the radio, which had been murmuring in the background. "What is this town?"

I said that a sign back on a highway overhang had read Crown Point. Crown Point, Indiana. The voice on the radio was delivering a loony commercial for a local hardware store. Curry turned the volume down.

"You hear the damnedest things on these little local radio stations. It takes about half an hour to drive across through the radio station's sphere of influence. Of course, at night you can hear them from half across the country. I remember hearing a Texas preacher in my Houston days, telling his listeners to send in their miracle requests and God, like a cosmic bellboy, would take care of whatever it was—you know, your business, your future. Then he went on to say, 'For those of you who have already sent in your miracle requests and didn't get your miracle, send in another request along with . . .' and I realized that he was suggesting that if a check was enclosed, maybe a bigger one than the first time around, it might help things.

"There's an interesting parallel to be suggested between this pie-in-the-sky theology that you hear in Texas—that God is around simply to grant your wishes—and the National Football League, which is the goal—'If I could make it with them, oh, please, Jesus!'—of a very large percentage of our young population, like those kids out there, and a substantial number of their elders, such as yourself, as well: getting into a uniform in the NFL would be like having your miracle request granted. They want it so much that they can taste it. A freaky number have actually deluded themselves into thinking it's possible. One guy came up to me in Houston one day and told me he was a better punter than Dan Pastorini; he knew he could kick better because he'd been in a touch football game one afternoon with Dan and he'd kicked a punt farther. 'I average about forty-six yards.' 'Well, if you can do that,' I said, 'you ought to come on out tomorrow, really.' He said, 'Well, I'm too little. I'm afraid I'd be scared. But I could do it!' He was this extraordinary combination of bravura and honesty. 'I *would* do it, too, but I'm just

. . . I only weigh 160 pounds and I'm just afraid I'd be . . . I'd be afraid.'

"People find the oddest excuses to become a part of it. One time Dan Pastorini and I were sitting in a place in Houston and this guy swooped down on us. Very obnoxious guy. He said, 'I can turn the Oilers around.'

" 'Well, do you want to be the coach?' I asked.

" 'Oh, no, I don't know anything about football. But I know how to *motivate* men. I could sell those guys on winning. I can turn the team around in one year.'

"I said, 'Well, why don't you call Sid Gillman? He's the general manager.'

" 'I'm going to.'

" 'Okay, fine,' I said, turning back to my drink.

"He leaned in again. 'I'm telling you, man, I can do it. I can do the public relations and everything—'

"Dan interrupted. 'Excuse me, but what we need's not PR.'

" 'Well, then, I'll stick to the motivating. That's what I truly am: a motivator. If I could just get in to see Gillman!'

"So I cried out, 'Call him. Call him! I'm sure he'll see you. Anybody that could turn the team around in one year . . .'

"The guy stuck around. He was inflamed with himself. 'I can motivate men. I don't need the money, you understand. I've got it made. I've got my own business. I'm selling winning! I can do it—that's what I sell.'

"I told Sid about him. I told him he could expect a call. Sid thanked me a lot.

"Actually, George, one of the aspects of football that makes it hard to quit is the relationship the player carries on with the fan. Something is built up by being out there in front of those large numbers of people . . . a love affair that an athlete carries on with his constituents up in the stands. When you contemplate that it's going to be taken away from you, you think that a large part of your identity will be a vacuum. At banquets it's very hard to sit out there in the crowd if you've spent a lot of time on the dais. That's why so many athletes say they want to get into public relations. They don't know what PR is except that it often puts you in front of a lot of people. Or they think of trying television. They want to be on television without understanding what it means to put on a three-minute sports show. There are even some guys who after they quit go into business and do very well; but six years later they'll be back in coaching. Why? With all its headaches and insecurity? Because this need develops over the years of play. A big part of an athlete's acceptance of himself is that he has thrilled people . . . and it is very hard to back away from that relationship.

"We had an Oiler fan—who described to me his ecstasy when we beat the Dallas Cowboys for our first victory in almost seventeen games. He said, 'You may think I'm crazy, but I was so happy at what you guys did that I went out and bought a bottle of champagne.' I thought to myself: Well, that's not unusual. But what he had done was take his shirt off, pop the cork off that bottle, and pour the champagne over his head right down to the last drop. He looked me straight in the eye as he told me this; he didn't crack a smile. 'I poured it all over me, because that's how good I felt.' I said, 'Gosh, that's terrific!'

"Where else in the world is it possible to get that sort of response from so many people? It just pours down from the stands. It sweeps over you. You can be out of sorts; you don't feel like playing. All of a sudden you're introduced in Baltimore Memorial Stadium. You run out across the grass, and the response almost lifts you off your feet. The emotion of that acceptance—all the more forceful because there's always the chance of rejection—is just the most extraordinary feeling in the world . . . an expression of a kind of . . . to me, it's love. If I had to pick a priority list for most of the players I know—and maybe they wouldn't articulate it the same way—I think that's the sensation that would be *numero uno*. Of course, there would be exceptions. Billy Parks, a great receiver with the Oilers, a deeply

110

sensitive person, would come over to me during a game and ask, 'What are these people doing here? Just *look* at 'em! They're crazy!' They'd be screaming down at Parks because his hair was too long and he had a reputation for being a radical thinker. He was very disturbed by the crowds. He hates it when they scream at the hard hitting; he doesn't feel they should be turned on by that. Billy'd say, 'Lookit those foolish people up there; their lives are so insipid that they have to resort to this for entertainment. Why can't they leave us alone?' Somebody in the stands would always be hollering down, 'Hey, Parks, you hippie! Whyncha go back to California! What the hell are ya doin' in Texas? Whyncha go home and grow pot!' Billy'd just sit there and he'd go, 'Oh, no. Gosh, I just can't believe it!' He referred to the owners as 'the latter-day robber barons.' He would play for living expenses, Billy would, just as long as the players got a chance to control their own destinies. He's a very idealistic young man, real refreshing, and even more naïve than I was. He thinks that society is so confused that the popularity of sports is one of the symptoms of our loss of perspective, our loss of proper ordering of priorities. He doesn't understand why people get rabid about it, why they take it so seriously. It's a game he loves, and he feels that we ought to be left alone to play it. He'd do that. He would play in that vacuum and enjoy it more."

"Would you ever do that—play the game in a vacuum?" I asked. "Do you have that sort of love for it?"

"My attitude is certainly more ambivalent," Curry said. "There are times when I hate the game. After all, it involves me with somewhat of an immature mentality . . . still playing a youngster's game at age thirty-two. Of course, it's my choice; the game doesn't make me stay . . . except that there are aspects that I love so much that I can't seem to get away. It's not the sort of choice you make in real life—leaving your family at a certain stage and stepping into the adult world. Because continuing on with football, I never left a family situation. It

111

evolved into the adult family community of players and coaches, the people that are the closest to me and have been through the years; and it's very hard just to walk away from them. Because that extension of the family is the best part. I can't tell you that I'm going to enjoy the two-a-days in Green Bay, Wisconsin. I can't imagine anything I'd less rather do. I dread it. I get butterflies thinking about it. It's going to be ridiculous, and I'm going to hate myself most of the time when I walk on the practice field, and wonder: What in the *hell* am I doing? And then we're going to win some silly exhibition game, and start pounding each other on the back, and I'm going to be like a little kid again. I'm going to be excited, exuberant, and it'll make up for everything."

"That's something I've always wondered," I said. "How much of it is for the money?"

Curry was adamant. "I'll guarantee you it's not for the money. One of the most aggravating things is the constant barrage that we're money-hungry. Since we have a very brief career it's true to an extent, and all of us want to do well financially, but there's not enough money to make a man go through what you go through to achieve excellence in professional football. There is not! Five hundred thousand dollars is not enough money—and I'm as serious as I can be—to go through some of the things we've been talking about . . . especially in the fourth quarter when it's ninety-nine degrees, a hundred percent humidity, and your legs feel like anvils—the right one won't go in front of the left—and you're behind by four points with thirty-five yards to go, and you *know* you've got to score, and Dick Butkus is standing there waiting for you . . . who has never been tired a moment in his whole life."

"Well, what is it, Bill? It's the big question, isn't it?"

"The main thing that makes me come back up to the ball is the fact that the guys next to me feel the same way I do, and I *know*, because I've seen them do it time and again, that they're going to come off the ball a little bit harder than they did the time before, *somehow,* with this reserve of strength or courage or moral fiber or commitment to each other or love or concern or whatever you want to call it—which means *I've* got to do it, if I want to be a part of this. That's what we had on the Colts and the Packers. So I will come back off the ball and I'll hit Mr. Butkus in the middle of his numbers with *all my might* again and again and again. But I'll guarantee you it's not for bucks! It's not for a fancy ring either. It's so that I can go back in the locker room, after having gone those last thirty-five yards and won the game, and walk back in there with my arm around Bob Vogel or Danny Sullivan or Tom Matte and know that we did that together, and that we both gave it a little more than we really had. Now, that may sound real phony. But I promise you it's the reason we play."

"What about those enormous sums athletes *are* being paid?"

Curry shrugged his shoulders. "Actually, if you look at the football players strictly in a business sense, by defining the number of dollars that he and his teammates generate, then they're not being overpaid. They receive a percentage of the revenues. As long as the owners are making a decent profit, and the fans are seeing a good product and don't mind paying the ticket prices, then athletes are not overpaid. Ticket prices are going higher, just like everything else in our society. Fans complain about it, but as long as they fill the stadiums, they shouldn't expect management to drop the prices. The first thing you learn in marketing is to price your goods at whatever the market will bear. There's a certain skill in determining the point of diminishing returns . . . just an old supply-and-demand curve. You can draw them up, plug the variables into the formula, and if you're skillful you'll learn how you can price your product. The NFL has demonstrated tremendous skill in this area. In Washington I think the top tickets now are eighteen dollars. And they *still* have a tremendous waiting list! How could you expect them to drop prices?"

"That's from the business perspective," I commented. "What

113

about in a social context, when you compare athletes' salaries to college professors'?"

"There's no argument that a teacher developing young minds or doing college research is more important," Curry said. "So it's difficult to reconcile that contradiction. It's one of the reasons that athletes are blamed and described en masse as 'overpaid egoists.' But I think football players should be considered for what it is that we contribute to the society. The most obvious, direct contribution is that we provide healthy entertainment. I've been a stronger advocate in the past about this when I had such an idealistic view of the game, strengthened, of course, by being associated with the Packers and the Colts. Now I worry more about the violence, or the intensity . . . whether that's healthy for either participant or observer. It does things to you—certainly the fan and often the player. Floyd Little over there at the Denver Broncos is going to night school and studying the law; he wants to become a juvenile-court judge. But a football helmet gets put on most any man and he becomes a sort of criminal himself.

"Probably, though, we provide a healthy outlet for a lot of the frustration that bothers people . . . especially in difficult times when people have a lot on their minds and really don't very much like what they do. So to be able to go out and scream at Bill Curry or Dick Butkus, or whoever you scream at or for . . . that kind of helps.

"There are other tangential benefits, like community pride. I think the Dolphins have helped Miami a lot. Miami was slipping into that Miami Beach image and struggling as a community. I think the Dolphins have really made a contribution down there. There's no telling what the Green Bay Packers have meant to Green Bay. The Colts of the sixties were an inspiration everywhere. We had a national following.

"And then there's the whole question of skill. Those of us who think we're good at what we do really enjoy watching someone who is a consummate expert. It's a great thrill to watch Arthur

Ashe at Wimbledon, or Jimmy Connors play tennis, no matter what you think of him. Whether you like Joe Namath or agree with his life style, he can throw a football, and it's beautiful. There's the artistic aspect: it's fun to watch; it's pretty. Gale Sayers just floating down the sidelines . . . it looks like he's not running fast, but nobody is gaining on him. Of course, dadgummit, I left out the artistic aspect until now because I play the least artistic of positions. A little play on words here: I am the butt of all jokes. Anytime I'm introduced, there's usually someone in the crowd who says, 'Turn around, Bill, we don't recognize you from the front.' You hear all the standard jokes about offensive centers. . . .

"In any case, the artistic aspect is a part of it. Beyond that, sports do something in this country that really isn't being done the way it should be in other institutions and in the private sector, which is that sports force people of different backgrounds and political persuasions and approaches to life to come together in a common enterprise. When you have sweated with a guy, and you have shared the horror of going down the drain, or when your efforts result in some sort of consummation, then you have the kind of relationship that can *only* come through combining sweat, tears, and blood. It may sound corny to say it that way, but that's exactly what football players do . . . in a most literal sense. So that after a while you get Bill Curry, who came from College Park, Georgia, who didn't understand black people at all, nor have any notion of what the real problem was, who, even having been brought up in a loving home, was certainly not enlightened with respect to the political or business or social problems that the black community had . . . gets thrown in with John Williams, from Toledo, Ohio, who understands very well what it means to be black, who has learned to cope with it. He is a very private person. But after several years of working together, he becomes a great friend. So that now I begin to get a glimmer of understanding. The same is true of John Mackey and Ray May and Bubba

115

Smith. It took me *years* of working very closely with these people to develop the mutual confidence required to open up and admit some of the problems and be honest about them. Athletics does that more quickly and more intensely than any other area in our society. I don't think it's stretching it at all to say that a youngster can sit out there in the stands and see John Williams and Bill Curry pat each other on the back after a game, or walk off the field together, talking about assignments, or working together hard . . . and for that youngster to get a subliminal kind of feeling: By golly, that's something I've never seen before. You know, a guy from Villa Rica, Georgia, has never seen a black guy and a white guy working together! There it is on television every Sunday. If he goes out to Atlanta Stadium, there it is, right there. So that when his buddies at school start talking about damn-nigger this and damn-nigger that, he's going to think twice: 'Now, Dave Hampton and Jim Mitchell are great Falcon players; they couldn't be what I've heard them called!'"

I stirred and said that I had always been startled by how little interaction there had seemed to be on the two teams I had been associated with—especially the Colts, where the blacks sat apart at meals and went to different places in town, and there truly seemed a division.

"Well, that's true," Curry said. "For all our talk of togetherness and the atmosphere of oneness and mutual respect . . . not much interaction off the field between the black and the white community. *On* the field it works. But it's just going to be a long time before the two subcultures really blend . . . even in athletics. Still, it's coming. Though the players come out of different backgrounds, they have more in common now than they used to. They pretty much like the same kind of music now; it used to be different. But it takes a long time to create even one relationship. It was four years before Bubba Smith looked at me one day and said, just a bolt out of the blue, 'You all right; you're a brother.' I could never have won him over by any overt effort;

116

just sitting down eating lunch and getting to know each other . . . that sort of thing.

"In Houston, Tody Smith, who was Bubba's younger brother, and Al Cowlings accepted me enough so that they decided they were going to teach me how to talk black dialect. I don't know if there's a way to articulate on a printed page how eloquent the black language can be. Even the black guys can't tell you how a particular word achieved its particular dominance in the vocabulary. There're lots of them, like *jive*. *Jive* is a big word; it refers to nonsense. 'Don't be jivin' with me, man, I'm serious now. I don't take no jive off nobody. I don't want no jive-talking in the huddle.' That sort of thing. It means: We're not going to put up with any nonsense, we're all serious about getting something done here. They'll refer to a guy who's not competent as a 'jive turkey.' 'You jive turkey! Don't you be comin' 'round here with your jive!' 'Ain't jivin', man.'

"The coach, by the black guys, was called 'co–ach.' 'Co–ach! Hey, Co–ach!' I don't know why that is. That's like that eccentricity of saying 'aks' instead of 'ask.' The black players don't say *d*'s; they substitute *t*'s. For instance, if you've got a player by the name of Rodney Jones, he'll be called Rotney Jones."

"You're a damn linguistics expert," I said admiringly.

"Well, I truly worked at it," Curry said. "Tody Smith and I had this routine. He'd come across me on the way to breakfast and he'd say, in this very arch WASP way, 'Well, Bill, top of the morning to you, how's it going, big fellow? Old chap.' Something like that. 'Cheerio. Nice to see your smiling countenance this morning.'

"So I'd try my response, which was supposed to be very hip black. I'd say, 'Hyeah, What it is, brotha man? Git it on!' It was about 1972 when the black guys first starting using that phrase: 'Hey, brother man, what it is?' The other one would say, 'I don' know, but it sure ain't funky.' So it got to be a game that Tody and I played all through the year. He'd say, 'Well, it's nice. I'm certainly having a marvelous time here in Houston, Texas. Always loved Texas.' He *hates* it with a passion.

"Tody would make me practice. It's not easy. I tried to teach other people how to do it, but it's almost impossible to teach. Fran Tarkenton wanted to learn very badly, and he tried endlessly to learn to say the one simple word they use so much . . . the way they say goddam. 'Gyat-daham, man!' He couldn't get it. He'd try; he worked at it for months.

"So at Houston we had a lot of fun with the whole language game, and if the black players were sitting around having a bull session, I was welcome to flop down and know that there was no uneasiness whatsoever. But if I had walked in and started saying, 'Yeah, hey, brother. Well, man, when I was growin' up, boy, down in College Park, Georgia . . .' you know there would've been an icy silence, because even though we got to be friends, we still realized where we came from. And you have to! I used to think that it was going to be an easy matter. When I came to Green Bay from the South I was so excited about coming to a place where there was no prejudice, but I soon found out that the black guys had difficulty finding a place to live up here. So I said to Marv Fleming one day—I was just going overboard to be friendly because I knew that I had to overcome this redneck label, being from where I was from—'I used to work for this colored fellow.' Marv's eyebrows went up and he looked at me. He said, 'Really? What color was he?' I just wilted. I said, 'All right, how do you want me to say it?' He said, 'It's *black.*' I said okay. And so I got to know him a little better, and months later we were talking about the situation in Watts in California. He was telling me how there'd been a lot of looting during the riots, that sort of thing, and he was describing what he knew of it. He said something about 'several colored guys.' I said, 'Excuse me, Marv . . . what color were those guys?' He tried to blush. He couldn't *believe* he had said it. But that was the beginning of my education, and he and I got to be pretty good friends."

I supposed that probably most good teams had a leader who helped bridge the differences.

"Oh, sure," said Curry. "A team has to have leadership that communicates well on both sides. In Baltimore, John Mackey was a great leader of men; so was Willie Davis at Green Bay. If a fellow wasn't getting to play, and he was saying, 'Well, I'm not being played because I'm black and the guy that's playing is white' . . . if John Mackey or Willie Davis walked up to someone like that, they'd say, 'The reason you're not playing is because you're not in shape, or because you're not good enough, and you'd better get good enough or you're not going to be here . . .' and there was very little the guy could do except work to improve himself. If a white coach or white player had said the same thing to him, it could've led to more conflict. That's not to suggest that either was a liaison or a go-between; both were strong leaders who assumed the role without being necessarily placed there. For instance, Willie Davis came up to me my first week in training camp at Green Bay. He told me that in the 1960 championship game against the Philadelphia Eagles, the first championship game that the Packers had been to in the Lombardi era, they had lost the game. As he left the field, he turned around and looked back out there; it was empty and people were filtering out of the stands. It occurred to him that he was leaving something on that field, namely regrets that he had not given the extra effort, the extra stint, that he had not pushed the extra ounce it took to get to the quarterback. And he was going to have to live with that the rest of his life, because there was no way he could recapture that moment. What Willie Davis said is that at that moment he made up his mind that he would never again look back at a football field and realize he had left some regrets out there. Then I began to watch and study him in practice and in games. Of course, if he had not told me the truth, it would've been very obvious to me because I was a football player and I could tell. He played twelve years; he never missed a game. I never saw him take a break on a play; I never saw him dog it or take it easy. Ahead or behind, it's easy to cruise when there's a wide disparity in the score. Davis never did. For him to take aside a young Southern white rookie and spend time like that is the sort of thing that began to cement us—black and white.

John Mackey down at Baltimore was not as verbal as Willie Davis. He was an outstanding player in terms of the incredible plays that he made . . . he would give the team a lift by doing those things. But he was also so forthright that he could head off such problems as a black player saying that he was being discriminated against because of his color. Mackey and Davis could provide the ingredients that bring factions together on a team and keep them from becoming split. Great intense players, not only as leaders but out on the field."

I wondered if the intensity Curry was speaking of might be part of the reason for the considerable number of black athletes.

"I think that's fair to say," Curry said. "The intensity of the black athlete is not untypical. I've heard people, with explanations about the length of the lower leg or the tendon and the Achilles or whatever . . . the strength of the hips or the conformation of the body. I don't know. But black kids coming along can run faster than white kids; I have seen hundreds of them and watched them on films. They can run faster! I think it's more because of their upbringing and their emphasis on sports, and that they have tougher lives than we do. When a white kid growing up in a middle-class community goes to Little League practice, his mama drives him over there; a black kid walks or runs. A white kid will have the extra thing to eat around the house; his mama buys cookies and junk food. Black kids don't eat unnecessary foods; they can't afford to go to the show and eat a box of popcorn and a bunch of malted chocolates, candies, and three Coca-Colas on Saturday afternoon. So black kids are harder physically, and tougher, more muscular, than white kids.

120

I'm not saying anything except *those* facts. You go down to the black community to talk to them or to their boys club or the YMCA, and those kids are out there eight, ten, twelve hours a day, practicing! They work at it harder because it's their way out. When I go to a group where white parents and kids are gathered, after my little talk, when it's question-and-answer period, they ask questions like: What's Unitas like? What kind of plays did you run against the New York Jets? Why didn't Earl Morrall throw the ball? All those questions. When I go to a black function, the kids raise their hands and ask: How much money do you make? How much money does John Unitas make? How do you make it in professional athletics? What do you have to do to be good enough? How fast do you have to run? What do I have to do to get up there and get outta here? That's what they're asking."

Chapter 11

We got talking about leaders and coaches, and Curry said that one of the problems with the Los Angeles Rams was that although they had a fine coach, there weren't any team leaders like Davis or Mackey . . . no real spark plug of a person.

"In Baltimore," Curry said, "we had about five. Sometimes Unitas; or Miller, or Mackey, or Vogel, or I. There were others."

"You'd better hope there's someone like that up in Green Bay."

Curry nodded. "Maybe up at Green Bay I can experience again the kind of camaraderie we had in Baltimore. I hope so. It was just a marvelous thing—this nebulous kind of thing that we call team spirit, or togetherness, or mutual concern, or even love, in rare circumstances. There has to be a precipitating substance, some agent that causes the kinetic energy to begin to pick up, so that things start to happen and the heat begins to radiate. Lombardi's function, as I think he saw it, was to be that—the agitator. He was the driving force. I wish I could remember my college chemistry well enough to pick out a precise formula. Hydrochloric acid mixed with almost anything creates heat. Or if you expose sodium to air, then it heats up, and becomes a brilliant, flaming thing. So Lombardi would've been that sort of agent.

"But there were other components in Green Bay. Willie Davis, who provided the bridge between whites and blacks; Bart Starr, who was a stabilizing influence . . . which was essential with Lombardi wielding the whip—the product could have exploded out of control and almost did a couple of times.

"Well, the Rams didn't have that sort of mix. Perhaps that's one reason why Carroll Rosenbloom picked me up. But to lead properly, you've got to be a starter, and you've got to be very proficient. You don't have to be an All-Pro, but there's never been a leader of a team who's done nothing but be on the suicide squad."

"How did *they* treat the fact that you'd been president of the Players Association?" I asked. "Like at Houston?"

"The coaches were very distant at first," Curry said. "I'm sure they all had some preconceived notions of what I would be like after the Players Association controversy. So I tried to rely on the old work ethic . . . to try to build a relationship based on the fact that I was there to contribute. So when the second- and third-stringers would be running the other team's plays—getting the Rams ready for the 49ers, that's what my job was—I tried to do it with a lot of enthusiasm and effort. On a team basis there was always genuine enthusiasm, but when you're trying to work up the necessary adrenaline to put some effort into running the 34 power sweep the way the San Francisco 49ers run it, then a lot of it is phony. It just has to be. So there was a lot of frustration. Many times I would catch—or at least I imagined it—an ex-Colt like John Williams watching me to see how I was getting through it.

"Early in the season Chuck Knox as the coach went out of his way to be friendly and to make me feel welcome; he was polite

123

and affable throughout. But naturally, as the pressure mounted and we got into the playoffs, his concentration was on getting the players ready . . . the guys that were going to play. So again I receded into the woodwork."

"Tell me about him."

"Chuck Knox is a history scholar from Juniata College in Huntingdon, Pennsylvania. He'd give us a quote from Homer every now and then. Very scholarly in his approach. He believes strongly in the power of the spoken word as a motivator; not the shouted word: he's not at all a screamer or anything of the sort. But he was a master of communicating his principles . . . little catchy phrases. 'Practice does not make perfect. Perfect practice makes perfect.' He would say it not once but time and again. And again and again. He believed strongly in repetition. His favorite was: 'Our pride and our conditioning are going to keep us in a game. And our toughness and our togetherness are going to win it for us.' He might stand there and say that four times in a row! No one tittered. It might be tittered at later, but not in his presence. He had these icy light-blue eyes; he looked right into the back of your mind—at least you imagined that he could. He believed strongly that if you said the same thing eight different ways, you're not going to get the same impact as you would by saying the same thing eight times the same way. A matter of teaching philosophy. Of course, Lombardi believed the same thing. 'Winning is not the most important thing—it's the *only* thing.' You might hear that *every day* for three weeks! Never deviated. That quote got bastardized into: 'Winning's not everything—it's the only thing.' I don't like that as much. That doesn't say it as well as the way I first learned it.

"Knox was like that. He believed strongly in the notion of repetition, and he had a very set routine. On Thursday, which was defensive day, he would come in and say, 'All right, what do we have to do on defense to beat the 49ers?' or whoever we were playing that week. He'd go through exactly what he thought we ought to do. Then he'd say, 'What do we have to do on offense to beat the 49ers?' Then he'd say, 'What do we have to do on the special teams?' and he'd go through it, A to Z. It might be very basic. He might say, 'In order to beat Denver you've gotta stop Floyd Little.' Everybody knows that. Sure, you've got to stop Floyd Little! When I first got to the Rams, I thought there might be a little snickering about that sort of thing; but there wasn't! When someone has the kind of personality that convinces you not only of his sincerity but of his competence, you don't laugh."

"I take it there wasn't much laughter *with* him either," I said.

Curry nodded. "Absolute absence of humor on the practice field. Pure serious business. Even if something happened that was really funny, and everybody would be chuckling out loud, I'd turn around and look at Knox. I never saw him laugh; he may have smiled, the corners of his mouth might've twitched . . . but just barely. Lance Rentzel ran into a wall one day. When something happens to Lance, it's always just disastrous. So it's not surprising that when he gets wrapped up in practice, he doesn't just sprain an ankle or trip over a yard marker or something. He ran full tilt into a twelve-foot-high, three-foot-thick concrete wall at the end of our field, running after a pass. And it was funny! I mean, everybody gasped: My gosh! Did he break his neck? Then when he got up, the laughter started, and it grew into a sort of crescendo until everybody was just doubled over, not so much because it happened, but because it was Lance. Well, Knox . . . I don't think so; not even a cute remark. This business of preparing a football club, to him, is very serious business, and he worked at it like a corporation president.

"We worked. We trained at Long Beach. A lovely facility, with the coaches' offices on the golf course. It was the hardest-working team I've ever played for, that means including Lombardi, Shula, McCafferty, or any of them . . . except for high school, when Bill Badgett used to kill us in College Park, Georgia. Good grief. From the first day I was there I was in pads.

125

I just went ahead and put 'em on; I felt like it was my only chance to make the team.

"The atmosphere differed radically from anything I'd been involved with before. I was not a team leader; in fact, I was not even a starter. No matter how much everybody likes a player, or how much they want to be friendly with him, it's a real strain on relationships when one guy is contributing and playing good football every week and the other guy's sitting on the bench. It's a dull strain: the guy who's not playing—especially if he's a person who *has* contributed—can't help wondering if the other guys consider him sort of like a relic. You ride down the freeway out there and you see one of those old cars somebody has parked because it's broken down, and when they come back the tires are gone, the steering wheel's gone, and it's just a hulk. Motor's still there but it can't be used anymore. I felt like a relic of that sort. It could have been all manufactured in my mind, or it could have been legitimate. I've seen it from the other side. I went through it with Tom Matte and John Mackey, two of my best friends, trying to make them *feel* like a part of the team, and you overdo it, which just adds to their problems. So now I've been through it on both sides of the fence. You find yourself not being able to concentrate on your assignments, your mind wanders. You keep wondering: What in the hell am I doing here? I'm just a drag, I shouldn't be around. So when you do get a chance to contribute, you're not ready. They stuck me in some games . . . in fact, I played half a game up in New York against the Jets. I did okay but it was not outstanding. I wasn't as prepared as I might have been. It turned out to be a very bizarre year in many respects.

"When they finally put me on the extra-point and field-goal team, I made some bad snaps, which was really disconcerting. On a Monday-night football game, we played the San Francisco 49ers. First time I had snapped the ball in a game in what seemed years! We scored in the first quarter, and I went out. I snapped the extra point; this tremendous roar went up. I knew something was wrong, and I looked up and I saw David Ray was trying to run for the extra point. When I came off, Chuck Knox met me at about the ten-yard line. He said, 'What happened?' I said, 'You tell me what happened,' because a center doesn't know; he snaps the ball and then everything disappears when the defensive people pounce on his head. I asked, 'Was it a bad snap?' He said, 'It hit halfway to the holder!'

"When I got to the sidelines, Elijah Pitts, my former teammate at Green Bay, came over. He was the team's special coach —the extra-point unit was his responsibility. I was just stunned! I've made bad snaps in my life, but never have I bounced one halfway to the holder! Elijah said, 'Why'd you do that to me?' I said, 'Elijah, I didn't do that to you. I did it to *me.*' He said, 'Oh? Right, right. I'll say you're right!' He was just upset.

"But from then on, a strange thing happened. The snap for extra points and field goals became like the four-foot putt to an aging golf pro . . . those guys who get the yips. Things that I had done when I was thirteen years old without even thinking about it, now suddenly were terrifying. It was really the strangest sensation. I'd stay out after practice and I'd snap literally hundreds of seven-yard snaps. In the past I might have done five or ten a day, and I never even thought about it. I'd lie awake and worry about whether I was going to make a bad snap. Finally I went along for several weeks, twenty or twenty-five snaps in a row without any trouble. Extra points and field goals. Then we got to the playoffs, and against the Redskins I made a high snap and once again our holder had to try to run with it. Fortunately, it didn't hurt us. We won the game. And then in the playoff game that we lost to Minnesota, I had a couple of snaps that were both okay. Of course, I'd much rather we'd have won the game and I'd had ten bad snaps.

"So it was a most unusual year. It could legitimately be said that I put the excitement back in the extra point for the Rams. I don't know if I was favoring my leg and had lost the physical stability on the snaps. I doubt it; I think it was more an emotional, traumatic thing. Maybe if I'd made a good snap on the first one, I wouldn't've ever thought anything else about it, and there wouldn't have been any trouble. What I guess it was . . . was a reaction against sitting on the bench."

I stirred in my seat and said that I never could hear about the agony of sitting on the bench without remembering a game I had gone to years before—a high school game, as I recalled— at which a woman in a seat directly behind me arrived late and as soon as she had got herself settled she said to her companion (her husband evidently), "For God's sake, where's Harry?"

Apparently they were talking about their son. I heard him say, "He's on the bench, dear. He's number eighty-eight."

"Eighty-eight? Is that Harry?"

He was seated at the far end of the bench, a very fat boy whose shoulder pads were bunched up around his neck, making him look as if he had been inserted between the leaves of a very large sandwich board displaying his number.

The game went on. Harry was evidently a sub, or perhaps a specialist, or even crippled; whichever, he never budged as the defensive and offensive platoons streamed back and forth from the bench. He sat stolidly in place, with the four eyes of the 88 staring up at us in the stands until finally the woman could take it no longer. She shouted down at him past my ear: "Harry, don't just sit there. For God's sake, *do something!*"

Curry roared at the story. "Yes, I know all about that," he said. "You're all dressed up and you have the feeling of people staring at you and you feel utterly useless. I know just what that woman was complaining about. . . .

128

Chapter 12

"Hey," Curry said. "Did you see that sign pointing to Gary, Indiana? 'City on the Move,' it said. We should note that we're passing Alex Karras's home town. Have you heard from him recently?"

"He was on the phone the other day," I said. "At one point in the conversation he said, 'I never met a man I didn't like except one, and that was Will Rogers.'"

"Typical."

"What was it like to play him?" I asked.

"What I remember most about Karras playing defensive tackle," Curry said, "was the shock, the *idea* that he could get past you to rush the passers. You couldn't imagine how he could get out of that little squatty stance of his with that little body and just blow by."

"He was a big talker in the line," I said.

"Alex usually had something to say when he made his tackle," Curry said. "He was always standing over the quarterback, saying, 'How did you like that one? Pretty good shot, wasn't it, Bart? Want me to hit you again? This donkey you've got on pass protection's not going to stop me.' One time he tackled Jerry Hill. Hill never said anything to anyone all season long, certainly not during a game. Very quiet. The two of them were lying at the bottom of a pile, just nose to nose, locked together, and Alex said, 'Well, Jerry, you still can't run, can you?' Jerry said, 'I don't know about that, but your breath sure does stink.' That got the whole pile laughing. They were just stacked up against each other, heaving and guffawing.

"We went to Detroit to play one day. Jerry Kramer always had trouble with Alex Karras on the pass block, and Jerry'd be the first to admit it, as indeed Alex had been the first to say it to everybody, too. So we worked out a deal where on pass blocking I would help block on Alex. Because of poor vision, with no idea what was going on on the field except by his great instinct, for Alex it was all playing against pressure. The plan was that I would block over onto him and he would think that it was a running play, a trap, because I would be coming aggressively at him. Meanwhile Jerry would take a step back and check my responsibility, who was the middle linebacker, Mike Lucci. Well, Alex would spin off to play the trap up the middle. Meanwhile Bart was set up and throwing the ball. We had a real good day. We really thrashed them, 31 to 7 or something, and this technique worked all day long. Alex never tackled the quarterback. Just the year before, the Lions had set a league record against us by tackling Bart eleven times, with the crowning blow a safety in the last minute of the game with Roger Brown, all three hundred pounds of him, sitting on Bart in the end zone. So we were pretty excited about what we had done. The reporters flocked around Jerry after the game and they said, 'Oh, what a great game you had on Karras; you just did a phenomenal job.' Jerry was very kind. He said, 'No, our young center, Bill Curry, is really progressing now. We worked out a system between the two of us this week that would help me with Alex. And it worked. I'm very proud of him. Bill just did a hell of a job.' So all that came out in the papers. It was quite a triumph for me. The beginning of confidence.

"So at Tuesday-morning meeting Lombardi walked in and he said, 'All right, we had a pretty good game. We beat the Lions. But I want to say one thing. If there are plaudits to be handed out, if there is to be an analysis of anybody's progress on this team, you guys don't make those analyses. I am the coach and I'll decide if somebody's progressing and if anybody's playing well. You understand that? Kramer?' 'Yessir.' End of discussion.

"We always seemed to have barn-burners against the Lions. We were playing Detroit one time in 1965, my rookie year, and they were just *whaling* us. By the end of the first half it was 21 to 3 for the Lions. Their third touchdown was on a pass interception; they ran it into the end zone. The benches are on the same side of the field in Tiger Stadium, and as Alex Karras came walking back up the field, he glanced over and noticed Lombardi standing there, just livid with rage because they were stomping us so. Alex said, 'Hey! How ya like that, ya fat wop!' Lombardi actually laughed.

"None of the rest of us did. We were terrified. We couldn't imagine what he was going to do in the locker room. The mortal fear we all had of Lombardi was pervasive in half-time situations. We *thought* there had to be some sort of explosion; it was like sitting on a time bomb. Half time is about twenty minutes. We sat and waited. Lombardi conferred with his quarterbacks; he moved around and did the little arrangements a coach does. The referee stuck his head in the door and gave us the five-minute warning; still nothing had happened. Then he stood in front of us, and we thought gratefully that the tirade couldn't last too long because we were due out on the field to get on with the nightmare. It was very short. Just one line. He said simply, "Men, we are the Green Bay Packers." We followed him out the door, and out there on the field we just turned the tables. I don't know if relief can be a motivator, but the team just *annihilated* the Lions—two eighty-yard passes, the offensive line coming off the ball, everything going the way you dream it should go. As the rookie center, my job was to trot in, touchdown after touchdown, and snap the ball for extra-point kick. Across the way Joe Schmidt, the Lion middle linebacker, was getting more and more agitated, screaming at his defensive team as things got worse. He was calling Alex Karras and Roger Brown all these terrible names. After the last point was kicked, clinching the game for us, he hit me late and we began to flail and swing. Frankly, it didn't even occur to me who he was. Out of the corner of my eye I could see Karras and Brown moving in. They weren't coming too quickly; after all, Schmidt had really been letting them have it verbally. Lionel Aldridge, my own teammate, tackled me and I remember being awfully relieved, as he smothered me down to the ground. But that was nothing to the relief I felt when I found out on the sidelines that the fellow I had been trying to mix it with was Joe Schmidt. I was mortified. . . . Let's see, Schmidt was gone when you played with us against the Lions. He was the coach. You didn't have to worry about him."

"That's right," I said. "Mike Lucci was the middle linebacker. He had purple eyes. You could see them above the bar of his helmet."

"How good a quarterback were you?" Curry suddenly asked. "I mean, I *know*, but how did your stats work out?"

"Well, let's see," I said. "When I did those four plays with the Detroit Lions I lost twenty-odd yards—most of them when I ran into Roger Brown, just like going into a wall. I churned up against him, my feet going like a comic bicyclist's. Certainly I wasn't going anywhere. But then that time in Ann Arbor when I was playing with you Colts against the Lions, I picked up twenty-three yards, fifteen of those, you'll remember, on a roughing-the-passer penalty."

"Oh, my God, yes," Curry said. "Mitchell. That big defensive end. He saw you standing there and came up and poleaxed you."

"Quite right."

"Twenty-three yards. Well, you're improving," Curry said.

I watched the fields slip by, thinking back on it, remembering the sense of inadequacy, and the miasma of hatred up on the line, and my wonder that any quarterback could feel at ease attempting to perform.

"Bill, suppose you put together a composite superquarterback?"

"A superquarterback. Different parts from the very best?"

"Right."

"Present company excepted."

"Present quarterbacks excluded," I said.

Curry thought for a while. "Well, to begin with, you'd have to give him Fran Tarkenton's feet. Football, like almost every game that involves movement, requires superb foot movement; there's not a position on the field that you can play well without being able to move your feet. If you move them very rapidly you'll be a back; less quickly and you'll be a linebacker . . . but always great foot movement is mandatory. Tarkenton is just shocking, he's so quick with his feet. There's just reams of film showing him evading people because of that skill. So I'd give our composite quarterback Tarkenton's feet. I'd also give him Tarkenton's ability to communicate. If he's telling you how to run a play, he'll do it not only verbally but with hand motions, walking through it, flailing his arms to show you exactly how it's going to work, and where the opposing player will be—drawing the whole operation in the air. He's an *exciting* conversationalist. Even at home he can't sit still to tell you something; he leaps up. Now, of course he can't call plays in a game so graphically . . . but it's terribly helpful in practice and in pregame meetings. All of this generates what Ray Nitschke called 'ent'usiasm'

. . . and getting 'ment'ly ready.' Tarkenton is a motivator . . . a promoter.

"You'd also have to give our composite quarterback what Alex Hawkins would call Tarkenton's 'perennial vision.' It's almost like a sixth sense—his peripheral awareness. People watching say: My gosh, how did Tarkenton know that Gino Marchetti was bearing down on him from behind? Fran tells us he's not sure why he knows, but I think he can just see the guy quicker than anyone else. The proof that he quite obviously sees more of the field is that he's completed more passes than anyone else in NFL history, utilizing what experts call an ordinary arm. In fact, Sammy Baugh said about that arm back in Fran's early days with the New York Giants that Tarkenton could really be a great quarterback if he could only throw. I love to tease him about that.

"On with our composite. Before his knees got horrendous, I don't think anybody ever dropped back to set up to pass better than Joe Namath. Those beautiful, nimble feet carrying him back. Then, I don't know if anybody ever got rid of the ball any quicker than Namath. A wonderfully quick release. If he can get rid of the ball in 3.1 seconds instead of 3.5, that makes my job at center a whole lot easier. It probably means the difference as to whether he's going to get creamed or not . . . four or five tenths of a second being a very long time when Merlin Olsen is pounding on a center's deviated septum. So it's important, and I have to say, as much as I hated to lose to Joe Namath in that infamous Super Bowl game which I've described, that his set and his release are hard to beat.

"For uncanny accuracy, and especially under pressure, I'd have to say Unitas. Physically, of course, it didn't seem he could do anything . . . the way his shoulders were shaped, that ol' humpbacked, bowleggedy guy. But his ability to release the ball and complete it under intense pressure, with *absolute* disregard for his safety, with a body like that . . . well, it required more courage than from most—especially with a guy with Merlin's strength, or Bob Lilly's or Alan Page's, when they're coming and coming, impossible to stop them cold, so that a center's only hope was to steer them by the quarterback. As Merlin would go by, reaching and flailing and clawing at him from within two feet, he'd yell, 'John! John!' to distract him, get him to miss the throw or something . . . but Unitas would just hit it on the money again and again. After the game Merlin would talk to the reporters and say, 'I just can't understand it! Unitas will *not* flinch. Nothing fazes that man!' Well, I know that voice scared *me*. I'm up in his numbers, just inches from him, and Merlin's got a voice as vibrant as Laurence Olivier's or maybe stronger: *'John! John!'* and it would rattle my ear bones."

I was impressed. "He'd yell at him? Damn, that's something. I think if I'd heard a player yelling at me, 'George! George!' I'd have turned around and asked, 'What? What can I do for you?' "

"You'd only have done it once on a football field," Curry said with a grin. "Concentration. That's what Unitas had. A lot of his success and poise was because he just worked so darn hard. Same way with Bart Starr. Just incredible hard workers! Staying out there hour after hour. The stories are legion and legendary about Unitas and Raymond Berry, but they're all true. For forty-five minutes or an hour after a three-hour practice, they stayed out and did the same pass routes over and over. I really believe you could've blindfolded Unitas—and for that matter Raymond, because Raymond couldn't see anyhow, and John would've dropped back the precise number of steps, turned and thrown, and he would've got the ball to Raymond Berry just the same. John Unitas . . . I think the reason he stayed out there was that he loved practice. He loved the games; he loved the training camp; he loved everything! John Unitas would have played linebacker if they had told him to. And he'd be playing football today if he hadn't got hurt. I guess he loved it perhaps more than anybody I've ever known."

"What sort of physiques would you give our composite?" I asked.

"Certainly not Unitas's," Curry replied. "Of the quarterbacks I've played with, we'd have to give our composite Pastorini's physique. He's just six foot three and he's strong; he's perfectly conditioned and he has a good tan and he has long hair and he's pretty the way a quarterback's supposed to be. Alex Karras would hate him more than anybody. He's got white teeth, he doesn't pick his nose or blow hockers on the wall the way linemen do. If he could learn to clean up his language, he would be the perfect embodiment of what a quarterback should be. We'd have to take his rocket arm, too. I don't think I've ever seen anybody throw it farther. Or harder. When he was a rookie he threw the five-yard look-in the same way he threw the forty-yard out, and we were surprised not to have Billy Parks come back to the huddle with the point of the ball protruding from his rib cage."

"What about hands?" I asked. I was curious about how much difference there was in how a quarterback's hands felt against him in the coupled stance of the center and the T-formation quarterback.

Curry thought for a moment. "There's always a lot of joking about hands when you're a center. At banquets when people ask what was Unitas really like, or Bart Starr, the center's stock response is that, well, Unitas's hands were fine, but Bart's were awful cold . . . that sort of facetious stuff. Actually, their hands *are* distinctive. I remember in the Senior Bowl I was surprised at how close and far under Joe Namath reaches, so that it's easy to snap the ball to him: the center just lifts the ball and he's got it. Bart Starr, on the other hand, stayed back, so that a little arm extension was necessary. Unitas was somewhere between Starr and Namath. I always felt that from the technical standpoint, there was much less chance of a missed exchange or a bobbled ball if I could feel where the quarterback's hands were. There was an incredible play, which happened in 1965 when I was with the Packers and we were playing the Colts . . . when Unitas stepped back from his center, Dick Szymanski, a beat too soon, and Dick centered the ball straight up in the air about six feet. Joe Fortunato was blitzing on the play and he plucked the ball out of the air and went for a touchdown. He got Szymanski's snap just as cleanly as if he'd been the quarterback rather than Unitas."

I whistled and said I could scarcely imagine such a humiliation.

"Well, that sort of thing doesn't happen every day," Curry said.

"What about game strategy and play calling?" I went on.

"Bart Starr would be the guy," Curry said. "He runs the game. He's studied for so many hours that it just seemed that every time he called the play, it was the right one. If something broke down, it always turned out that one of us had committed an error, rather than Bart making the wrong call against the wrong defense. Great strategist. Bart didn't have fantastic physical ability. Sometimes he got battered up because we didn't do a good job of protecting him. But he had this phenomenal knowledge and grasp of what we were trying to accomplish; and not only that, he made us believe. If there was ever a doubt in Bart's mind, he was the only one that knew it. With some of the other quarterbacks, you can see that flicker of indecision when they call the play. All that detracts.

"Bart Starr's was the strongest personality of the quarterbacks I played with. Unitas had this charismatic way of carrying himself, but he didn't have the presence of Bart in the huddle. Bart was in total command . . . his authority over personnel, even Vince Lombardi. He was the *master* in the huddle. Lombardi'd stick his head in the huddle at practice, but Bart would say, 'Just a minute,' in that gentlemanly fashion of his. 'I'm calling a play here.' He was a perfectionist. I remember on one occasion Lombardi was castigating us for a bad game, and he mentioned that only Willie Davis had had enough courage to come up and admit that he hadn't played well. Bart Starr interrupted him and stood up to say that if the Coach thought about it, he'd remember that he, too, had come up and remarked on how badly he'd done. Lombardi had to stand corrected. All of this, of course, made a great impression on the rest of us. The respect we had for him was really enhanced by this sort of thing.

"Does that finish up our composite quarterback?" Curry asked. "Hey, hold on!" He lifted his hand off the steering wheel and snapped his fingers. "I would say our composite quarterback should definitely have a big toe like Earl Morrall's. He doesn't have one. He had the courage to test his new lawnmower with his foot, and that year he came back to training camp without his big toe. It improved him as a quarterback. Not only did it demonstrate to us that he had great courage, but it improved his spiral. Prior to that, he had always thrown what they call a nose-down football, which is hard to catch. But now, when he pushes off with that toe missing, it makes him lurch forward, the nose of the ball pointed up, and it's much easier to catch. So the receivers appreciated the lawnmower. I forget exactly what brand it was, but it just did a great job on Earl. The missing toe didn't help his running much, which was questionable to begin with; afterward he tended to list toward the side that had the toe missing."

Chapter 13

I guess it was Earl Morrall's missing toe that got us a little farther up the road (I remember passing a road sign that read Hobart, Indiana), putting together a composite of the NFL's worst physical specimen—lifting parts from great athletes who had succeeded in the league despite physical limitations.

"Look at your old pal Alex Karras," Curry said. "The amazing thing about his great play as a Lion tackle was that he couldn't see what he was doing . . . worst pair of eyes in the NFL. He got to the quarterback by a sort of touch system."

"He refused to wear contact lenses," I remembered. "He tried it once and didn't like what he saw out there on the playing field. He told me once that he had come off the field with the defensive unit and sat down on the bench next to Bill Swain, the linebacker, who it turned out had just lost his contact lenses. They joked about it: 'Hey, do you think we're facing in the right direction?'"

Curry laughed. "Yes, you'd have to give Karras the vote for the worst eyes."

I told Curry that Karras had once told me who had the worst breath in the NFL.

"What?"

"The worst breath. It belonged to an Italian who played in the line for the Los Angeles Rams—Joe Scibelli. Karras said that for the first three years Scibelli relied *very* heavily on his bad breath until, of course, he developed into a great player. Then he didn't have to breathe on people that much."

"Karras told you that?" Curry asked.

"That's right."

"Well, I tell you who had the worst feet. Bubba Smith. The worst feet I ever saw in my *life* belonged to Bubba Smith. They're about twenty-three inches long and sort of conically shaped. Remember those pointy-toed shoes that people wore years ago? Well, Bubba's feet were made for those . . . they'd just slide right in there. He has yellow toenails that crumple under, and they're all wrinkled and just *horrid*-looking. Both feet are perfectly flat; he has no arch whatsoever. He just stands flat down on the floor."

We drove on for a while until the steady consideration of Bubba Smith's feet got to me and I said, "Let's move on up the body. Who had the worst calves?"

Curry said, "Well, the worst calves I ever saw—and you'll remember I can only speak of experience with four NFL teams —belonged to Rick Volk, who played safety for the Colts. Definitely. It was obvious from the day he got to the Colts that somebody had 'rustled his calves.' "

I made an appropriate snort of dismay. Curry apologized and continued about Volk. "He had a powerfully built upper body . . . with a face straight out of the Vienna Boys' Choir; you'd expect to see him with one of those little candle-snuffers that acolytes carry. But he's never had any calves! We got on him about it. The only thing he could counter with was: 'Have you ever seen a thoroughbred with big calves?' That was the best he could do."

"What about knees?" I asked. I remembered Gil Mains, a Detroit Lion tackle I'd known who had been hurt in a game against San Francisco and whose knee looked as though a pillow had been sewn into it.

Curry said, "I guess Taz Anderson, who played for the St. Louis Cardinals and the Falcons, really had the worst knees in captivity. He had ten knee operations; they'd taken so much out that the last time they went in they actually found a metal clamp that somebody had left—one of the doctors along the way."

"It isn't easy to talk about knees," I said, conscious of Curry's problem with his.

He shrugged. "The pain is always there, but it's not gruesome, and it doesn't keep you from functioning."

"What about thighs?" I asked, to change the subject.

Curry shifted in his seat. "This is painful," he said. *"I've* probably got the worst thighs of any NFL player. People meet me. 'This is Bill Curry. He played center for the Baltimore Colts and the Green Bay Packers.' They're impressed. But if I happen to have on shorts and they look at my legs, they get this real suspicious look. I just don't have big thighs. Never have."

"Do you know the Ronald Searle caricatures?" I asked. "The long, thin legs and the tanklike bodies on top?"

"I hadn't thought of myself quite *that* way," Curry replied.

"What about hips?" I asked.

"Worst hips go to Don Shinnick," Curry said. "Shinnick did not have any hips. "Do you know about him?"

"No," I admitted. "You mentioned him as one of the Colts' physical misfits."

"That's right. He played linebacker for us. He's practically a composite bad body himself. Shinnick had the worst body in the history of the world. His lower stomach protruded; his chest had fallen early in life; his shoulders sloped down to these hairy arms that reached below his knees. He not only had this bad body, but hell, he has a bad *mind* . . . as witness that he's now defensive coach for the Oakland Raiders. But Shinnick did things like . . . one day Gale Sayers of the Bears broke into the clear. He was running for a touchdown, and Shinnick was in his normal position: seated on his rear. He was looking downfield, like a man seated on a beach staring out to sea. In the game films you could see him: he raised his right hand very carefully and with his forefinger he fired at Sayers all the way down the field like this: Bang! Bang! Bang! That actually happened. That Tuesday the coaches ran the film over and over, unbelieving. He missed, though. Sayers went in for the touchdown.

"Another thing that happened. The year before I joined the Colts, Shinnick was in a game against the Atlanta Falcons. On this one particular play there was a turnover, a fumble or something, and the Falcons took over the ball. They called a sweep, and immediately ran for about ten or fifteen yards. Shinnick was on the sidelines, jumping up and down and screaming, 'Come on, let's go! Let's go! What's wrong? Let's go! Let's pick it up out there! Don't let 'em run like that!' Somebody finally said, 'Shinnick, they just ran around *your* side. You're supposed to be in the game.' We're playing a man short. He was standing there screaming. He was the starting linebacker and he had just forgotten to go in the game! The legend was that as he rushed on the field, struggling to get his helmet on, somebody on the defensive team turned around and shouted, 'Go back! Go back! We'd rather do it without you!' "

"Goodness. I don't believe it," I said frankly.

Curry looked over and grinned. "The thing about Shinnick stories is that you're better off telling *lies* about him because nobody believes the truth. Listen to this one. In 1968 we were in Yankee Stadium against the Giants. Shinnick had pulled a hamstring muscle—which was understandable because it was the only muscle in that body of his. But he had been healing for about four weeks, and Shula wanted to give him a little play so he'd be ready for the playoffs. We were beating the Giants pretty bad. Shinnick didn't know he was going to be put in the game. With about four minutes left to play, Shula looked down the bench and he called out, 'Shinnick! Shinnick, get ready!'

"Well, Shinnick was standing there, having undone his belt buckle on his football pants and put the belt through his head-gear—behind the bar of his face mask—and then buckled it back together so that he wouldn't have to hold the headgear. It was hanging there in front of him off his belt. He had a warm-up jacket on and he was eating a sandwich, standing there in the sun enjoying the game. When Shula began to yell, he stripped off his jacket. As he ran onto the field he was trying to get his helmet off the belt without dropping his pants in front of sixty thousand people. When he finally got on the field, the Giants were just breaking the huddle. He got the defensive assignment from the middle linebacker, and as he lined up in front of the tight end, he discovered to his horror that he was still holding the sandwich in his hand. He turned and handed it to Roy Hilton, the defensive end. Roy turned next door and stuck it in the defensive tackle's—Freddy Miller's—hand. Why Freddy didn't just throw it on the ground I don't know, but with one hand down in his stance, he reached out with the other, wiggling it behind him to try to set the referee to take the sandwich. The referee stood there, you know, with his mouth hanging open."

"What finally happened to the sandwich?" I couldn't resist asking.

"Damned if I know," Curry answered. "Somebody probably ate it . . . very likely Fred Miller, who was a big eater and had ahold of the sandwich anyway."

"How good a player was Shinnick?" I asked. I didn't under-stand how anyone like that could survive in the NFL.

"It was crazy," Curry said, "but Shinnick led the league for years in interceptions . . . mostly because he was in the wrong place at the right time. A quarterback would read the defense perfectly, set up to throw where there *had* to be an open man, just automatic, and there, as if a twelfth player had materialized, would be the grotesque figure of Shinnick. He gambled; he improvised, and it would pay off."

I thought for a while and asked, "Where are we on our composite? Shinnick has thrown me off."

"Is it stomachs?" Curry suggested.

"Stomachs!" I said. "Whose stomach would our composite have?"

"Stomachs," Curry reflected. "Highly competitive area here, though when I came in the league in 1965 it was fashionable to have a flat stomach. Vince Lombardi once said that he'd never seen a mean fat guy and certainly he wouldn't tolerate any fat people on *his* team. On the Packers, Ron Kostelnik had a tendency to balloon up, and so did a guard named Dan Grimm. Before weigh-ins—and they'd get fined if they were overweight —they wouldn't eat for two days and they'd step up on the scales, these troubled men with their eyes deep back in their heads, and afterward they'd spring for their lockers, where they'd wolf down a couple of apples they'd hidden back there —just leaning back and dropping them down their throats like pills.

"Their fat problem possessed them, like people in love, and they were always tinkering with ways to solve it. John Mackey of the Colts, who also tended to balloon, used to scout scales beforehand; he'd find that if he stood up in the left-hand corner he'd weigh a third of a pound less. So then he'd get a teammate to stand alongside him on the opposite side of the coach who was weighing him in, and this guy just at the right moment would lift Mackey up with a finger under his elbow—they rehearsed all this beforehand, doing it very quickly and subtly— and the scale would read 220. If John Sandusky, who was the coach handling the weigh-in, was in a good mood, he'd say, 'Okay, John, 220', but if he was testy that day he'd make John stand in the middle of the scale and he'd move everyone back;

John would weigh 224 and he'd pay a fine."

"The largest I ever saw was Roger Brown of the Lions," I said. "Three hundred pounds. After practice the coaches'd send him out to run off the fat. He wore leatherlike sweat suits and he'd run through the sprinkler systems set out on the practice fields and you could hear the wet suit slapping against his skin."

"Damn, I never saw him fat," Curry was saying. "Actually, you don't look across the line in the NFL and see fat people. Brown's weight was concentrated in those enormous thighs of his. Tree trunks. The first time I ever saw him, I came up on the ball from our huddle and I looked to the right and left; all I could see was Brown: he filled my field of vision."

I said that Brown had once told me that the nicest part of football was a bath with Epsom salts that his wife prepared for him after a game. He would ease himself into it and groan with pleasure. I had always imagined, because he was so big, that all that was required was a couple of pails of water in the bottom of the tub, and when he squeezed himself in, it would flow around him right up to his chin.

Curry suddenly snapped his fingers. "I know who's got our stomach. John Williams! With the Colts and now with the Rams. It bellies *way* out! Oh, yes. Big protruding abdomen. But actually he had an excuse for it. He said it was due to a congenital defect he had in his back. The coaches would look at him and shake their heads and he'd say, 'Coach, I'm not overweight, I'm just *sway-backed!*'" Curry laughed. "Great football player . . . but a very odd body."

"What about the chest?" I asked. "That's next."

"Shinnick again," Curry said. "He didn't have a chest. He had a breastbone, but no chest. He didn't have a neck either. We called him No-Neck. So he takes care of the entire upper torso of our composite."

"I wonder how he'll like that," I commented.

"He always got kidded a lot. Actually, he was a dedicated player on the field and especially off—charity work, that sort of thing. Kids love him. 'Crazy Shinnick,' they called him. He was a curiously sensitive man. He was offended by the language that we used in our discussions. In fact, he would leave the room if we used foul words. But he loved long in-depth discussions, so he made up new words for some of the terrible ones we were using. He substituted various sorts of vegetables and fruits for parts of the anatomy. Instead of the male organ and all the slang names for that, he wanted us to call it the 'onion.' That way we could go ahead with our conversation without his being so ... compromised, and he could say the words and enter into the discussion. To top it off, he's extremely religious, a fundamental Christian."

"The onion?"

"That's right. The onion."

"What about a football mind?" I asked. "Who was splendidly deficient in that department?"

Curry thought for a while and then he said, "Well, Allen Jacobs, bless his heart, had great football ability but not much football sense. He ended being traded from Green Bay to the New York Giants. He was a fullback, and very strong . . . built like Jimmy Taylor. Just a real powerful kid, but he kept running into his own people and smashing them around. He studied his plays all night long, but then he'd get flustered. When Lombardi screamed at him, he'd get very uptight and he'd contract, and shrink, and what he'd learned was just squeezed out of his head. He'd get the general idea, but then on a reverse play he'd run over the quarterback who was handing him the ball, just *crush* him, and then he'd run down his interference and step on Jerry Kramer or Fuzzy Thurston, his own offensive teammates, and knock them down and bowl them over; but then, because he had such a lot of talent, he'd run over a couple of linebackers and a safety. He'd come back to the huddle shaking his head, and even Lombardi couldn't jump on him. It tickled Lombardi. He'd shake his head and remark that Jacobs would be considered his best offensive asset if he didn't destroy so many of the offensive platoon as he went along.

"I'll tell you another one," Curry said, "and you'll appreciate this from your time with the Colts. Glenn Ressler, great guard. He was Dean's List from Penn State and yet he never could remember the snap count. Unitas would always give it as the last item in his play call in the huddle, but almost instantaneously Glenn would forget. On the way up to the line of scrimmage he'd bump into me and ask, 'What's the snap count?' 'Two,' I'd whisper. This happened about twenty-five times a game, and it went on for six years. I'd say, 'Dammit, Glenn, *listen,* and in the huddle he'd give me this big wink and smirk to let me know that this time he was *really* going to concentrate and remember. But then on the way up he'd lean in: 'Hey, what's the snap count?' Finally, after four years of this, in this one game against Pittsburgh we got far ahead, and when Ressler came up and whispered, 'What's the snap count?' I said, 'I don't know.' He was frantic. 'Jeezus, come on, *tell* me,' because if an offensive man doesn't know when the center is going to snap the ball, he's going to get clobbered by the man opposite. Up on the line he began cussing. Ressler must have been smoked by Ben McGee, a big old tough guy who played defensive tackle for the Steelers. I remember Glenn's cussing, because I could hear it along with the quarterback's signals."

I leaned back and considered our composite. "That's an awful specimen we've put together," I said.

"But it's worth mentioning," Curry commented, "that you could send our composite out on the field—Bubba's feet, Volk's calves, Anderson's knees, my thighs, Williams's stomach, Shinnick's chest, and Scibelli's bad breath, Karras's eyesight, Jacobs' football sense and so forth, and yet you might have a helluva football player out there. It's surprising how often an oddly conformed player can be a superb athlete. Take Ted Hendricks, the Mad Stork, who played for us in Baltimore, and is now with Oakland. Six foot seven inches tall, and only 210 pounds—our second-draft choice from the University of Miami, and when he arrived in training camp we all said there's no place in our business for a guy built like that. He'd get killed. He looked like a series of toothpicks—all those long pipelike extremities. But then you began to see people working against him. It was as if they were running into a wrought-iron structure like a playground Jungle gym, which *looks* delicate, but of course isn't, and these guys would slam into the Stork and sort of slide off him to the ground. When he moved, it seemed very slow, like you could stand around and watch this strange creature try to put one foot in front of the other, but then he'd be *by* you, flapping at the quarterback with those long whippy macaroni arms. He's the best outside linebacker in the business."

"So there's hope for us," I said.

"What's that?" Curry asked.

"I mean for those of us who are not perfect physical specimens.

Curry looked over and laughed. "Anyone interested in playing football who looks in the mirror and doesn't especially like what he's looking at shouldn't worry. After all, he might have a really awesome bad breath to start work with. There's always hope."

Chapter 14

We were by-passing Chicago for Lake Forest, where we thought we'd drop in on a Chicago Bears practice, moving along swiftly without too much traffic on the expressway, when suddenly Curry took a glance into his rear-view mirror and yelped. I looked back, expecting the revolving lights on a police car, and was startled, too—at the sight of the grille of a big rig filling the mirror. He was perhaps a foot behind our tail.

Curry speeded up and we drew away from him. "Damn, look at him, right behind us. What the hell are you supposed to do? Ever since I started driving a small car, truckdrivers do that to me . . . just creep up on me, inches away, at fifty-five miles per hour, and I look in my rear-view mirror and it reads MACK. It just fills up the mirror. Or it says WHITE TRUCK, or INTERNATIONAL. That's the thing about the truckdrivers; what the hell am I supposed to do?"

"They get bored," I suggested. "Maybe it's the drugs I hear many of them take . . . just to get through that interminable dull

149

time. Maybe it makes them a bit crazy."

"It wouldn't surprise me," Curry said. He kept glancing up in the mirror. It took him a few minutes to recover. "I guess whatever the profession, you find people taking drugs when they're under stress . . . housewives, doctors. Truckdrivers. I shouldn't be too surprised. It's the same in football.

I said I had wondered about that. Did he take drugs himself?

He said he had experimented. "You take a small dosage of Dexedrine. If you're not in great shape, if you need a little pepper-upper to speed up your cardiovascular system, then it'll probably improve your efficiency a little bit. If you're in excellent shape it probably won't help you at all. It'll make you think you're playing well when in fact you're not. It can screw up your timing to some extent. Your mind's just going so rapidly! . . . Didn't you take them for studying for exams and stuff like that?"

I told him that I was always too nervous about it—afraid that I'd walk into the examination hall and look in my brain and there'd be nothing there.

"Have you ever drunk six cups of coffee on an empty stomach?" Curry asked. "That's the feeling. It's a pleasant high, and it makes you enjoy things that you ordinarily wouldn't enjoy, like the National Anthem. You stand out there on the field and really appreciate it. 'Hey, wasn't that great!' That's the feeling. It always makes you think you're doing just fine. You come off the field and say, 'Gosh, I'm just having a great game! I'm killing the guy!' Then you watch the films two days later and you discover that he just ate you alive."

"I would think that knowing that, you'd give them up pronto."

"Well, there was another reason for taking them," Curry explained. "What happens with me and a lot of other players is that on the day of the game you actually get depressed; you start thinking: God, what am I doing here? This is crazy! I'm thirty-one years old, I'm out here still playing this stupid game. I ought to be selling insurance. That's the sort of thing that starts to run through your mind when you see guys at a pregame meal sitting there trying to get themselves ready, staring at the wall, or Mike Curtis in the locker room rocking to the music, taped, bandaged, padded to the gills three hours before game time. So you can take a pill early, and it sort of gets you excited about the game when you otherwise might not be at all excited.

"My family doctor, who's the team doctor for the Falcons, said, 'Bill, we don't know what those things do. If I were prescribing a pill like that for a housewife who's going on a diet, I could project with some degree of accuracy because I would run the tests on her heart and her cardiovascular—the EKGs and EEGs—and how it affects mental processes and that sort of thing. But we don't have any research to tell us what these pills do to a body that is heavily muscled, which already puts a big strain on the cardiovascular system. When that body is subjected to intense stress in a football game, or is suddenly pounced upon by six hundred pounds or eight hundred pounds of weight, suddenly thrust down like that . . . we don't know what might happen. It's just not worth the risk because of the uncertainty.'

"That made a lot of sense to me. So I dropped it. There were times when I would lapse back because it was a good crutch, it was a good feeling, it got you motivated, pepped up. But I quit fooling with it." He glanced up into the rear-view mirror. "I wish those truckers would," he said.

We reached the Lake Forest turnoff without being molested again. Curry had said that the Chicago Bears trained there at a lovely college, a very carefully groomed place, with Tudor buildings, ivy-covered, little signs set on the lawn under the trees to tell what variety they were, and it just boggled his mind to think that the Bears were let loose in that place every year about that time. What a gang!

"There *is* something about the Bears, isn't there?" I offered. "I mean, that reputation has remained exactly the same."

"The Bears were *always* a weird team to play against," Curry said, as we drove down an avenue through sun patches under the big shade trees. "To begin with, their uniforms are funny-looking, their helmets curiously shaped plastic throwbacks to the old leather variety—they look like black kitchen pots without the handles—and they always had four or five guys on defense who wore high tops, which made them look as if they'd stepped out of the past. The Monsters of the Midway. You could always bet that those players with the high tops would take a couple of cheap shots. And then they were always a very verbal team, cussing and carrying on . . . against us, themselves, the refs, anyone. Very noisy. I remember the first time I played against them was in a preseason game in 1965—a Shrine game between the Packers and the Bears in Milwaukee. Just before we went out, Ray Nitschke came up. That was a surprise. Veterans didn't talk to rookies, especially Ray Nitschke. He said, 'Look, if you happen to make a play over near the Bears bench today, just get up and hurry back to the huddle.' What the hell was he talking about? Did they have knives over there? I nodded politely and asked if he could explain. 'There's a short, fat coach on this bench who's got a real loud mouth and you shouldn't hear that kind of stuff.' Nitschke was looking me right in the eye, not a tremor in his face to suggest he was kidding. 'I don't want you *exposed* to that kind of filth.'

"Actually, you didn't have to get near the Chicago bench to hear him—he was impossible to escape anywhere on the field. Last year he was out somewhere beyond those elms exercising those incredible vocal cords."

We parked the Volvo and walked down to the practice field. Curry was right. The campus was lovely. Water sprinklers ticked back and forth. I thought of the newly arrived coeds, coming in from summer vacations, setting out along the gravel walks from their rooms, where they had just unpacked their bags (setting up their keepsakes on the bureau tops), wandering across the grounds congratulating themselves on choosing such a beautiful college to spend four years at and idly wondering if Lake Forest had a nice *choir* they could join, or at least a pretty alma mater song they could sing at jolly-ups—when suddenly, *boom!* They were gang-tackled by that foul voice storming up from the practice field.

We sat in a small wooden bleachers to watch the practice. Curry was nervous about being there. He whispered to me that if he was recognized by a Bears coach he'd either be taken for a spy from the Green Bay Packers or—even worse—identified as the president of the Players Association. Neither possibility was pleasant. He was quite uncomfortable.

We did see one extraordinary episode before we left. Just in front of us a rookie Bears place-kicker was practicing kickoffs; the rest of the squad was at the far end of the field. He must have felt quite fine not being under the scrutiny of any coach and knowing that our little bleachers crowd had only him to look at—you could tell by the way he set the ball up on its tee and the way he paced off his approach steps. He never looked at us. He made some tremendous kicks, one of them into a heavy stand of bushes at the end of the field, and we watched the rump of the Bears player down there trying to push his way in to find the football. But then on this one kick, trying to put another into the bushes, the place-kicker got his approach wrong, or slipped perhaps, so that his foot flew out, just ticking the top of the football, and he cartwheeled backward and landed on the flat of his back with a grunt we could hear from where we sat. The ball fell off the tee and rocked back and forth, perhaps a foot away. Our little crowd in the bleachers erupted. We bawled with laughter. I had once seen a quite decent golfer just tick a golf ball off the tee so that it actually rolled back up against the tee he was trying to hit it off . . . a great gutsy swing he had given it. But no one laughed. The Bear, however, being a professional, was a fair target. . . . We worshiped his pratfall, sniffling with pleasure, and I remember he leaped up, looking first at the far end of the field to check that no one there was witness to his embarrassment, and then he picked up the football and set it back on the tee with studied care, as if nothing more untoward had happened than that a gust of wind had blown it off. He never dared look at us.

Walking back to the car, Curry and I kept describing it to each other. As we drove off I said that I would never think of the Bears in quite the same way. Perhaps they would never again be so intimidating.

Curry said that would be very nice, that he would try it himself, but by the time we were back on the expressway he said it was no use: the Bears he would always think of were never a guy taking a pratfall but Doug Atkins and Dick Butkus. Damn. What a shame. He began talking about them.

"Doug Atkins just terrorized everybody. Bob Vogel of the Colts, who played opposite, lived in mortal fear of him. For his first game as a rookie with the Colts, he reported after the All-Star game and the team went down to New Orleans to play the Bears in an exhibition. He played against Doug that night, and they ended up having to pack Bob in ice; he almost died from hyperventilation and loss of water . . . dehydration and all that. Atkins just gave him a horrible beating, just *destroyed* him. Bob said he finally got out of the ice, dragged himself into the shower, got himself dressed, and staggered onto the team bus; when he got back to the hotel he wandered into the dining room and was having a beer or something, and this huge shadow blotted everything out—somebody coming up behind him. He turned around and it was Atkins. He told me he almost passed out. He said, 'My gosh, you've found me here!' His first impulse was that Atkins had come to finish the job. Actually, big Doug had come over to tell him that he'd done a pretty good job for a rookie . . . which Bob still considers his greatest compliment as a professional.

"Atkins was quite a character besides. He brought pistols to the Bears training camp. One year some of the rookies were

154

upstairs playing their stereo in a room right above Doug. He hollered up there, saying, 'Hey, turn that thing down.' They didn't hear him, so he hollered again: *Turn that thing down up there!'* Still nothing happened, so he just picked up his .38 and fired four shots through the ceiling. Just fired away . . . and that was the end of the music for *that* year.

"The first time I saw him was out in San Diego where New Orleans—the Bears traded him there—used to have their training camp. Right before the Colts game against San Diego, we were getting dressed and I saw Doug walk in. I didn't know him personally. I just gawked at him. He was six foot nine and you just couldn't believe his body! He looked like Michelangelo's *David,* just a perfect body. He had about twenty-one-inch biceps like, as Mike Curtis would say, 'tumorous arms.' When he flexed them the muscle was just awesome. Bob Vogel was leaning over in his locker, picking up some pads. Doug walked over and stuck his bare arm down in front of Bob's nose and flexed the muscle. Vogel just fell over backward. He didn't even have to look up to see who it was. It scared him half to death, though we were playing the Chargers that night and he didn't have to go against Doug. Bob was really funny, talking about Atkins. Even in the late stages of Atkins's career, when he had lost speed, he could pick Bob Vogel up, great as Bob was, and somehow he would catch him under his shoulder pads and run him straight to the quarterback and just throw the both of them down in a great heap. There was nothing Bob could do about it."

I asked, "Bill, why did the Bears ever get rid of him to New Orleans?"

"Very odd," Curry said. "He was too independent for George Halas, their coach. Billy Martin, a friend of mine from Georgia Tech, used to play with the Bears, and he said that Halas would come out to practice at training camp and he'd look around and call out, 'Where's Doug?' The Bears' practice field at Rensselaer, which we went by a while back, bordered right on a farm.

Well, they'd finally find Doug over there with a baseball hat on, wearing his pads and everything, and he'd be sitting up on a tractor going out across the field, just plowing up furrows. He had these odd yens and he'd just go ahead and do what he felt like. Or back in Chicago, Halas would come out to practice at Wrigley Field and he'd call out, 'Where the hell is Doug?' Doug would be sitting up on the old wood scoreboard, putting numbers up, sliding different numbers into the slots, putting up different scores. . . . I guess the Bears couldn't stand that kind of behavior. He was whatever he wanted to be, just like the joke: 'Where does a four-hundred-pound gorilla sleep?' 'Anywhere he wants to.'

"So they sent him to New Orleans for the last couple of years. What match-ups he was involved in! The Colts said that when Jim Parker was playing left tackle and they played the Bears, Szymanski would snap the ball and when the play started it was almost as if twenty guys on both teams would stop and watch these two Goliaths smashing into each other, Jim Parker and Doug Atkins. What a physical match! *Boom! Boom! Boom!* All day. Doug would be over there just tearing heads off, and of course Parker would be getting his licks on Doug. One day Alex Sandusky, who used to play a very good guard—in fact, Alex Karras said in your *Mad Ducks and Bears* that Sandusky was probably the best guard he played against—hollered something over at Atkins: 'You big bastard, you think you're tough. Well, don't you ever line up over *here;* you'll be sorry!' So the Colts scored pretty soon after that. When they came up for the extra point, Doug walked right over and took his stance in front of Sandusky and when the ball was snapped, he hit him *and* Szymanski playing center next door and he just flipped them end over end at the kicker and upside down, turned their helmets around and everything. Szymanski, for the rest of his career, used to tell Sandusky that if he ever challenged Atkins again, he'd better make sure he did it by himself. He wasn't going to be around."

"What about Butkus?" I asked. "He's a Bear one thinks of."

"It was a hostile, terrifying presence that he exuded," Curry said. "A ferocious unpleasantness . . . almost as if it were a physical odor. Now, I don't mean to suggest that Dick has chronic body odor—although Lord, he probably has—but that there was a mystique about him you had to defeat as well as Butkus the player. He once played against me in a way so completely out of character that I wondered if he wasn't doing it to startle me into a bad afternoon. It started at the coin toss. Normally he was just strictly aloof: you looked across at those *eyes*. But this time he was grinning from ear to ear and looking at the ground. He wouldn't look me in the eye. Everything seemed very funny to him. During the coin toss he stood there pawing at the dirt like a kid, giggling, and I half expected him to squat down and draw up a play for his teammates in a get-up game. It all seemed so completely out of place . . . and it continued all during the game. I'd come off the line and fire at him, and rather than throwing me to the ground or smashing me in the head, the way he usually did, he would evade the block, and in the pileups I could hear him snickering and giggling as if we were all tumbling around in a girls'-dormitory pillow fight. Once he reached over and tried to unsnap my chin strap, roaring with laughter: 'Bill, there's something wrong with your helmet' . . . a crazy sort of fun-and-games attitude which caught me and everyone else off guard.

"But that wasn't the way he usually was. Oh, no. There was that 1969 game against the Colts that the Bears were trying desperately to win for Brian Piccolo; they had just heard that week that he had cancer. We'd heard rumors before the game. I didn't actually know until after the game, when I asked Butkus and Dick Evey and they said yes, it was true. Certainly everybody on the Bears was playing all out that day, and although we had a much better football team than Chicago, we were struggling. Our bread-and-butter play was an off-tackle trap, which was set up so that both John Mackey, the All-Pro tight end, and

I would block on Butkus; in theory it was supposed to be pretty rough on him. This one time I went out and hit him right, just at the numbers, and as he was fighting me off, Mackey came flying across from his position and tried to put his headgear through the earhole of Butkus's helmet. Terrible crack! Butkus went down, but then he jumped up and seemed to go berserk. He started screaming, 'Don't you hit me like that! What do you think you're doing? Don't you dare hit me like that!'

"We both stepped back. It was as if we'd committed some awful outrage on him, an indignity which didn't belong in football. I'm sure that's what he wanted us to think . . . so we wouldn't hit him like that again for fear of retaliation. He's probably made it work on players, and I've *seen* it work on referees . . . Butkus in a pile and wrenching the ball away from the running back, lying there on the ground and then jumping up, holding it out, and shouting, 'You better give us this ball. It's our ball! Our ball!' and I've seen umpires gulp, staring at him mesmerized, and reverse themselves for the Bears."

"Did he ever punch you?" I asked.

"No, but Sam Huff of the Redskins did once. He reached into a pileup, lifted off my helmet like taking the lid off a pot, and he got me."

"Lord almighty," I said.

"I went berserk. Literally berserk. Which was just what he wanted me to do, because I was the only center available. My teammates had to restrain me."

"I'm surprised more people don't go amok," I said. "I would tend to if someone hit me . . . even a light tap. It's such an indignity. It'd be a pathetic gesture, but I'd do it."

Curry said that he felt most rages on an athletic field were the result of frustration. He described Bob Lilly of the Cowboys taking his helmet by the strap and flinging it up into the sky in disgust at Dallas' loss to the Colts in the Super Bowl. "It went nearly as high as a punt, turning way up there . . . but I guess he had good cause."

I said that I remembered Tommy Heinsohn, the coach of the Boston Celtics, doing something like that. He had taken a kick of frustration at the water bucket at one end of the bench, missed, and the shoe on his kicking foot, which was a large loafer, had come off and sailed up into the second balcony at the Boston Garden, where it caused a considerable stir since Heinsohn is a big man who wears a size 16 EEEE shoe.

"And of course golfers are bad," Curry mentioned. "They're always scaling their clubs into ponds."

We drove along for a while. I stirred and said that the most spectacular example of frustration I had ever heard of involved a sailing skipper who was so furious at the performance of his new Morgan 39, which is quite a respectable-sized yacht, that he sank her by running her into the side of the Chesapeake Bay ferry the *Chesapeake Queen.*

Curry was astounded. He looked over. "He did what?"

"He just plumb sank it," I said. "I've often thought of the captain of that ferryboat, and what he must have thought up there on the bridge, idly noting the Morgan coming on a course for him, reaching up after a while and blowing his ship's whistle a few times, thinking perhaps the skipper of the yacht had fallen asleep at the helm . . . but then coming to the side of the bridge and looking down and *seeing* him suddenly, red-faced and mottled with rage, just gone *amok*—that grand word—just amok in the stern of his boat, one hand on the tiller and beating at the deck with the other like a jockey, urging the Morgan into the iron walls of the ferry."

"Well, that's something," Curry said. "Did it sink?"

"Oh, I think so," I said.

"Well, there's the difference," Curry said. "The guy was finished with his Morgan. He never had to worry about the damn thing again. But the trouble with Butkus was that he was always surfacing against you. There was no way that you could get rid of this terrible source of frustration."

159

"Do you remember the first time you played against him?"
I asked.

"Oh, yes," Curry exclaimed. "The first time I had to play
against him was in Green Bay my second year, the first year that
I was a starter for the Packers. He was my primary responsibility. He literally destroyed me that day—emotionally, as well as
physically. I *could not block him* to save my life. The game was
close and very tense. At one especially important juncture we
ran an off-tackle play on first down; I hit Butkus, but not as well
as I should, and Jim Taylor couldn't break the play clean. Had
I made a good block on Dick, it probably would have gone for
a touchdown. As it was, Jim made nine yards before Butkus hit
him, and we were down inside the Bears' twenty-yard line. A
good position. Second down and one. On second down we tried
the same play, and this time I missed Butkus completely and he
stopped Jimmy for no gain. So now it's third and one. We tried
a reverse action play, a counteraction move. But as I fired out
at Butkus, he had sneaked up so close to the line of scrimmage
that he went around *behind* me and he made the tackle on the
line of scrimmage. Three plays in a row. So it was fourth and one
yard. Bratkowski was the quarterback because Bart Starr was
injured at the time, and Zeke called 'Quarterback sneak
straight ahead.' Butkus came up, lined up right on my nose, and
at the snap he stuffed me into the backfield, into Zeke, grabbed
both of us and wrestled us down. The Bears took over the
football.

"Fortunately, we won the game. But as we were coming off
the field, Dick was in a pretty good mood after this tremendous
performance, and he walked along talking with me . . . about
a mutual friend named Marty Shottenheimer and the fact that
he was getting married, or something. I had an eerie feeling, as
if some unseen presence was around. As I went into the locker
room I learned that Lombardi had been right behind us. Sure
enough, he came walking over, and without his normal anger
—he should have been mad at me because of my ineptness—

he simply said, 'Butkus really *owned* you today, didn't he?' There was a hurt in his voice rather than anger, the way he said it, and that made the impact all the more."

"And you had Tuesday and the game films to face," I said.

"Exactly," Curry said. "I doubt that I slept more than three or four hours between that Sunday afternoon and the following Tuesday morning. I was literally an emotional basket case. Carolyn had to coddle me and take me to the movies on Monday—the kind of things you do to youngsters who are going through traumatic times—anything to take my mind off the humiliation that I was expecting. I was *really* terrified. And the most amazing thing happened at the Tuesday meeting. As we neared the point in the game when the crucial series of downs was coming up . . . for the only time in the two years that I was in Green Bay, one play before it began, Coach Lombardi got a phone call. His father was ill, or something. He left the room; he turned the projector over to Ray Wietecha, who was the offensive line coach; as we went through that series, it was very obvious to everybody who had been defeated; but Ray Wietecha pointed it out without Lombardi's inclination or ability to scream and shout and generally terrify. I made it through there, and then Coach Lombardi reentered the room and we progressed, and nothing was ever said."

I asked Curry how much of the problem of playing against Butkus was psychological.

"Well, his physical talent was enormous," Curry said. "Tackles from sideline to sideline all day long, never a letup. But true, just to think about him was intimidating. I'd come up over the ball and instead of thinking: I'm going to take three steps at a forty-five-degree angle and cut him off and I'm going to knock his knees out from under him, I'd wonder: What's he going to do to me now? Where is he?"

"Wouldn't that be true of other great defensive stars?"

"For me, Butkus, and also Merlin Olsen of the Rams, were the people I never seemed able to cope with. I don't think any center in the history of football could consistently beat Butkus or Olsen. I don't think so. Merlin was so huge and big. You'd think that anybody that big could be cut at the legs. So I'd throw at his legs and he'd leap over me. Butkus'd do the same. It's the worst feeling there is when you commit yourself to that kind of block and you don't touch *anything!* You'd get those glances in the huddle. 'Can't you do something about that guy?' 'Yeah, I'll get him! I'll get him!' So the next time you decide to take him on, stick him right in the numbers with all your might. So you try that and he stuffs you right into the backfield. Before long, you get to feeling helpless: you've tried six different techniques and nothing's worked.

"At his best, prior to those injuries to his knees, Butkus was the greatest football player I have ever seen. It's almost as if the Creator in this particular case had sat down and said to himself: I am going to create the ideal middle linebacker . . . in terms of temperament, physical characteristics, and even physical appearance, especially on the field. Awesome. He was a startling player to watch at full speed. Almost every game he'd do something that you just never thought anybody would do. He would run up and scream at you; he'd go a whole game and never say a word; he might stand pat for a whole game until the ball was snapped; he might run and jump at you at a time when you didn't expect it; he might lay back on punt snaps for a whole game and wait for you to try to come down the field, where he'd destroy you physically; or he might lay back at that same position and as you looked back to snap the ball, by the time you'd looked up he'd got a ten-yard running head start and he'd just knock you unconscious at the line of scrimmage. Never knew what he was going to do!"

I said the Bears player we had seen falling down trying to kick the ball was beginning to fade as a symbol of the Bears.

"Of course. A *Butkus* is a Bear," Curry said. "Mind you, there were some normal people on that team. Sensible, prudent people. Larry Morris was a great linebacker with the Bears; he was the defensive captain of the team. He had to snap for punts. They were playing the Lions one day. He came out to snap for this punt on fourth and four and he had a little trick he decided to pull. A lot of centers have done it; I've tried it, but I've never had it work. You squeeze the ball right quick, without moving it, and sometimes you get a guy to jump offsides. So they came out and it was fourth and four. Roger Brown, the Lions' three-hundred-pound defensive tackle, used to line up in front of the snapper. So Larry did his little move and Roger jumped offsides and the referee threw the flag. Roger started to scream, 'You son-of-a-gun, you pulled me offsides, you tricked me!' Larry said, 'Hey, shut your mouth, fatso,' or something like that, something very unlike Larry Morris, who is one of the world's nicest people, a real gentleman. But he said it, as he tells the story, and maybe a couple of other things that he shouldn't've said . . . because it was going to be a first down and the game was almost over, and the regular center was going to be coming in. Well, Morris, to his horror, was left in at that position and he had to snap the ball again; there was Roger standing there, lined up in his stance, with that meathook of his, the forearm, all the way back behind his hip from where he was going to unleash it, and he was saying, 'I'm going to kill you.' Larry figured out what he was going to do. He said the films of the play were great—both the Lions and the Bears played it over and over at their meetings—because it showed that as he snapped . . . even *before* he finished snapping the ball, he did a ninety-degree left turn for the bench. He never made any attempt to block, and Roger Brown chased him clear to the Bear bench and through the Bear players and over the bench before Larry escaped."

I laughed and said that I had rarely heard of a better example of prudence. "So they're not only Dick Butkuses's."

"Larry was not only one of the more prudent of the Bears," Curry went on, "he had other things on his mind besides football, which was not common for that crowd. He has an insurance agency along with a real estate business. Fran Tarkenton

163

was one of his clients; he handled his car insurance. The Bears and the Vikings were playing in the last game of the season that year and Tarkenton had somebody drive his car from Minneapolis to Chicago; after the game he was going to drive it down to Atlanta, which is his home town. But on the way from Minneapolis to Chicago, the kid he'd got to drive wrecked the car. Fran found out about it just before the game. So when he walked out onto the field for the coin toss as the offensive captain for the Vikings, there to meet him was Larry Morris, the defensive captain of the Bears. They met at midfield. Fran said, 'Larry, c'mere, I've got to ask you something!' So he pulled Larry aside and he said, 'What should I do about the car? This kid wrecked it and it's sitting here in Chicago.'

"Larry heard some more details and he said, 'Okay, get a couple of estimates, go ahead and get it fixed up and then just send us the bill.'

"By then the referee had made the coin toss and the two captains jogged back to the bench. Coach Halas took Larry by the arm and asked, 'Larry, are we kicking or receiving?'

"Larry said, 'I dunno, Coach.'

"Halas said, 'What!'

" 'Honest, Coach,' Morris said, 'I have no idea.'

" 'You mean you don't know who won the damn toss?'

"Morris shook his head. He said, 'No, you'll have to ask the other guy.' "

Chapter 15

We spent the night in the Pfister Hotel in Milwaukee. It was an interesting evening because we ran into Don Drysdale, the cranelike ex-Dodger pitcher, who was working on the California Angels broadcasting team and had been in the booth at the ball park that afternoon for an Angels-Milwaukee game. Curry recognized him crossing the lobby and the three of us sat down in a corner of the hotel's taproom.

They exchanged news. Curry talked about going back to Green Bay and he admitted to Drysdale that he was worried about making it. He talked about what the injury with the Houston Oilers had done to his leg, and that he had no idea how the hamstring was going to hold up. Maybe the decision would be made for him very quickly.

Drysdale grinned, and with the avuncular attitude of someone who has already gone through it, he said that in his case it had been a very easy decision to make—and a very quick one.

Curry winced slightly and said he wanted to hear about it.

Well, the fellow who made it easy for him was Roberto Clemente, the great Puerto Rican player for the Pittsburgh Pirates. Clemente always gave him fits at the plate. Drysdale said that the distinguishing characteristic of Clemente's base hits was their ropelike trajectory—the ball hit at buzzing speeds—and every time he came up to bat against him Clemente seemed to hit the ball up through the middle; he never could see him come up to the plate without thinking of the terrible thing that had happened to Herb Score, the Indians' pitcher, when Gil McDougald hit the ball back into his face and almost blinded him. He'd stand on the mound and look down at Clemente and the Score thing would pop into his mind and he'd give an involuntary shudder. It got so bad, Drysdale told us, that when he delivered the ball, he flinched at his follow-through and tucked his head down a bit.

Sure enough, Clemente came up against him and drilled one.

Curry interrupted to ask if a pitcher could get any indication of where the ball was going by the sound it made coming off the bat.

Drysdale said it was possible—one got a *sense* of where it was going, and indeed at the crack of Clemente's bat he had tucked his head down just a bit more. It was a base-hit line drive into center field. He told us he could hear the ball hum by his ear. Then he had the sensation of a bug crawling on his neck; he reached and flicked at it. Leaning down for the rosin bag, he noticed a runny substance on his finger, and still feeling the irritation, he reached up and discovered his ear was bleeding. The ball had actually taken the skin off the top of his ear on its way out to center field.

"Incredible," Curry said. "Incredible."

Drysdale told us that the next pitch he threw in that game was to Manny Sanguillen, the Pirates catcher, who had poled the ball out of the park in deep left field. It was the last pitch Don ever threw in the major leagues. There was a quiz going on up on the electric scoreboard . . . and when he turned around to stare gloomily after the ball Sanguillen had hit, he noticed the scoreboard was flashing the answer to whatever it had asked in a previous inning: ROBERTO CLEMENTE, it read in big letters.

"I remember the first game I pitched in the majors," Drysdale said, "and the last one, and I'm telling you I remember the last one better."

I went up to bed early, leaving the two of them gossiping in the taproom. I remember remarking to myself how affected Curry had been by Drysdale's story. He had said, "Incredible," a number of times, staring at Drysdale as if he had survived going over the top at Ypres . . . and it had seemed odd to me that anyone who spent his Sunday afternoons facing down the likes of Merlin Olsen and Mean Joe Greene, the great concussive sweep of stiff-arm blocks, and who himself had almost had a knee destroyed, should be so overwhelmed by a nick off a man's ear.

But then it occurred to me that the question of his career coming to an end, perhaps not just then, but soon enough, was something that he could not help picking at, like a sore. The average athlete began to wonder when his career was going to end almost as soon as it started—knowing that it could either be shortened with devastating swiftness by an injury, or eventually reach the point at which the great skills began to erode. As time went on, and the broadcasters began to refer to the athlete as a "veteran" and the club began to use high draft choices to acquire young collegians to groom for his position, a player like Curry had to decide whether to cut it clean and retire at the top —as Rocky Marciano did—or wait for some sad moment—Willie Mays stumbling around in the outfield reaches of Candlestick Park—when the evidence was clear, not only to the player but to his peers, that the time was up.

Bubba Smith, the great Baltimore defensive end, had described the process to me as being symbolized by a small, monkeylike figure he called "Rigor"—"Mr. Rigor Mortis"—who sometimes reached up out of the grass and slowed his getting to the ball-carrier. Smith told me once, "And then one year he jumps on your back. Sometimes you can brush him off, but every year he gets heavier and grips harder. I've seen him riding the backs of others. He's right around here somewhere. Look yonder—he might be behind the door. Maybe he's behind that curtain over there."

The next morning Curry and I left the hotel early, planning to be in Green Bay before noon. Bill seemed preoccupied and he kept referring back to Drysdale's story of the evening before.

I asked Curry if moments like that were likely to come along in football—excluding a sudden injury—a moment, like Drysdale's nicked ear, when a player knew he was finished.

"I'm not so sure you can tell so easily," Bill said. "But you can tell. The difference is perhaps half a step in speed. . . . Just several weeks of not quite getting there would tell you. I won't know until I get in a couple of exhibition games."

We drove along in silence for a while—the countryside, green and beginning to shimmer in the July heat, slipping by.

"Curious," Curry said. "I can never think of the Pfister Hotel back there without remembering Ray Nitschke—who was about the best middle linebacker there ever was—at the end of *his* career."

"He was a friend of yours?" I asked innocently.

"Friend?" Curry's hand came off the wheel and made a fist. I thought he was going to punch it down on the horn.

"What was wrong with him?" I asked. "He was a teammate."

"He was just about the embodiment of my despair at Green Bay," Curry said. "That's one part of it. The other may be more interesting. You've been asking me about the qualities that seem to turn up in great players. In his case he was driven by an intensity which was simply demonic. I don't know another way of describing it. I remember Dan Pastorini, when I was with the Oilers, telling me about Nitschke's intensity even during the *coin toss* at the beginning of an Oiler-Packer game. The captains were all standing out there at the fifty-yard line. Nitschke was out there jawing at the referee who was going to flip the coin: 'All right, goddammit! Come on, ref, toss the goddam coin . . . let's get it over with. I want the hell out of here! Let's get this game going!' He really frightened Pastorini," Curry said. "There were certain people in football like that who harnessed and used rage. Lombardi, of course. Nitschke. Mike Ditka. Mike Curtis. Dick Butkus. When they got near you, they scared you . . . the way you knew certain pitchers—like Sal Maglie—would throw a fast ball under your chin. No joy at all playing people like that. They performed with what some people called ultimate intensity'. . . others—Lombardi—'hatred.' Of course, you could be great without it. Merlin Olsen burned with intensity, but he'd help you off the ground after knocking you down. Mean Joe Greene of the Steelers, despite his name, was always messing around pleasantly: "What's happenin'. What it is, brother man? How's the wife?"

"Did you feel this fear the first time you met Nitschke?" I asked.

"What happened was a complete reversal of attitude," Curry said. "I remember the first time I was ever aware of him was on television—that famous freezing day in 1962 in Yankee Stadium when the Packers played the Giants . . . a colder day, they told me when I joined the team later, than anyone on the club could ever remember, far worse than even the awesome cold that sweeps in from the lake at Green Bay. I didn't know who Nitschke was. He hadn't been a starter until that year. But every time I looked, there was number 66 in that quick crablike shuffle across the field to smash down the Giant runners . . . voted the most valuable player that afternoon. Then a couple of days later I happened to catch a glimpse of him as a mystery guest on *What's My Line*—talk about how conditioned we are by TV!—and I could hardly believe what I was looking at:

glasses, gentlemanly, professorial demeanor, that high, balding dome. The panel didn't come close to guessing what his profession was.

"Then I met him for the first time personally when I was taken out to Dallas in 1964 to sign a Packer contract. I was in absolute awe . . . he was so massive and powerful. He kept most of my attention throughout the game that day. I watched him and Dan Currie warm up together on the sidelines and I remember being amazed that they threw passes at each other . . . such an odd way for linebackers to get ready.

"But then when I got to Green Bay, it was a different matter. The awe got to be tempered by a sort of hatred. At practices he'd appear on the field padded up to the hilt—forearms, hands, everything—and you got to know it was going to be a long, tough day. Sometimes things got so bad that Jerry Kramer, Bob Skoronski, Fuzzy Thurston, and Forrest Gregg would gang up and beat the daylights out of him just to slow him up—because he'd run around clotheslining people and crashing into them, even the quarterbacks. He'd be always yelling in that rough, nagging voice of his, 'Come on, let's have some ent'usiasm . . . let's get ment'ly. . . .' He came from Chicago somewhere. . . . Just a constant stream of chatter until finally Lombardi—although he liked a lot of spirit—would call out:

" 'Hey, Nitschke . . .'

" 'Yes, sir?'

" 'Shaddup.'

"But what he was . . . well, he was Lombardi's instrument to instill fear. The sort of thing Lombardi would say was this: 'I'm going to use fear on you guys; it motivates you. I'm going to make you afraid. I know you're not afraid of the physical aspects of football or you wouldn't be here. You're not afraid of scrimmaging or anything like that. But you *are* afraid of embarrassment in front of your peers. That's what I'm going to do to you. I'm going to embarrass you, humiliate you . . . until you do the job.''

170

"I didn't really know what Lombardi was talking about until one day he said, 'Well, now we're going to have a blitz drill.' I noticed Ken Bowman, who was the starting center that year, looking kind of askance at me out of the corner of his eye. I wasn't especially bothered. A blitz drill to me just meant: Okay, a middle linebacker's gonna come running in on a blitz, and I'm gonna have to hit him . . . that's the way the game goes. As a center you have to be able to do that to protect the passer.

"So Ray Nitschke lined up opposite me. In the drill, the center is supposed to drop straight back about three yards, set his feet, and then hit the middle linebacker, who's coming in full speed. I wasn't afraid of Ray Nitschke. But that first time I was hit was the hardest I'd ever been in my life. He knocked me down. A little stunned, I got up and I thought: Well, *I'll* hit *him* that way next time. But I couldn't seem to do it! It's a skill that it takes time to cultivate, to drop back that quickly and get your feet set, and I wasn't good at it from the technical standpoint. Of course, Nitschke had some advantages. He was a veteran player and a great linebacker; also he knew the snap count and he knew the plays. Not only that, but he would jump the snap count. He'd come up close to the line of scrimmage and he'd be almost by me before I could hit him. Moreover, I was not allowed to cut him low in the legs because he had bad knees. I never did get to where I could block him on those plays. Once he broke my headgear with his forearm. On another occasion he snapped my chin strap . . . with just the sheer force of his blow. And every time Nitschke came, it seemed like he came harder . . . running over me and into the quarterback, and he'd scatter the backs and mess up the whole play. I couldn't get him. Every time I missed him, Lombardi would go into a tantrum: 'Goddammit, Curry, can't you move! Can't you do anything!' And then a strange thing happened: I began to dread those practice sessions with blitz drills—with a fear that I had never experienced before in my whole life. I suddenly understood about the fear that Lombardi said he was going to instill in us."

I asked Bill what would have happened if he'd gone to Lombardi and said, "Nitschke's beating the snap count on me. Why doesn't he play it square?!"

"Oh, boy!" Curry laughed. "If I'd done that, he would've said, "Son, I didn't ask you to come and tell me how to conduct drills. If you can't block him, then get your ass *off* the field! I don't ever want to see you again!' That's probably what he would've said.

"I did see Danny Grimm, a guard, lash out at him that way, and he got sent right off. Lombardi ordered him out. 'Get your ass outta here!' Grimm stood around and humbled himself and apologized about twenty-five times, and he was finally let back into the drills.

"But then afterward," Curry went on, "one day this strange thing happened with Nitschke. Do you know what a cut block is?"

I said that I wasn't sure.

"Well, you drive out at the man" Curry explained, "as if you were going to hit him about chest-high, and when he lunges to meet you with his forearm, you suddenly dip down and hit him around the knees and knock him down. That's a cut block. It's a technique that I've made a living off of for almost my whole career. Well, you don't do it in practice. It's just a . . . I started to say 'an unwritten rule,' but it's almost a *written* rule. You just *don't cut* your teammates; it's too dangerous to their knees. This day we were practicing running plays. Lombardi was always fussing around the huddle and sticking his head in. 'All right now, I want you to run a 36.' Bart didn't like that sort of thing. He'd say, 'Wait just a minute. I'm running this huddle.' And Lombardi would step back. But this time Lombardi stuck his head in and he stayed there. He said, 'Curry? I want you to cut Nitschke.' 'What!' He said, 'I want you to cut Nitschke down.'"

"Not only did Nitschke have a couple of bad knees, as I was

172

telling you, but he did not even have on any knee pads, or thigh pads! But what was I going to say to Lombardi? Nothing. I snapped the ball and I fired out and I cut Nitschke, really knocked him down. I thought he'd probably get up and just kill me; he'd kick me in the face or something. He didn't say a word. Everybody called, 'Hey, good block! That-a-way to git 'im,' 'cause everybody got mad at Ray during practice because he was always knocking everybody's head off. So I was kind of proud of myself and very relieved. I came back to the huddle beaming. Lombardi stood there. He wasn't smiling or anything. He said, 'Hit him again.' I just went pale. I said, 'Oh, no. Oh, Jeez, what . . .' So I went out, and I cut him down again. He did not say a word. When I got back Lombardi said, 'Now, see there? You got him.'

"So Lombardi would do things like that to try to build your confidence and to help you, I suppose, and also because maybe he felt that Nitschke needed a taste of that notion Lombardi had about fear."

"I like the way he never complained," I said.

Curry looked across at me. "That just made it harder," he said. "The rest of my time with Nitschke was a steady, humiliating, demeaning punishment. There was nothing I could do about it. All my life my reaction has been if you push me, or cross me, I'll fight. On the field I play at a high level of combativeness. It's just not civil out there. One afternoon Ray hit me lots; that was the day he snapped my chin strap. Then he hit me again. So I hit him and I started pushing at him . . . really the sort of preliminaries that invariably lead to a fistfight. But he wouldn't do me the honor of hitting back . . . he wouldn't deign to fight a rookie. He said, 'Kid, what the hell's wrong with you?' . . . like flicking off a mosquito. It just humiliated me . . . everybody looking on. I couldn't even get the satisfaction of getting whipped by this guy.

"Then after I had become a Colt we went to Green Bay in 1968 to play the Packers. I kept thinking of Nitschke. I told the

Baltimore coaching staff, 'I'll bet they're going to blitz a lot of the time because they think Nitschke can beat me.' They were skeptical, because according to their reports, the Packers only had a 5 percent blitz tendency, which meant that out of all their defensive plays, you could expect them to blitz only 5 percent of the time, and only very rarely with the middle linebacker. Of course, I was hoping they'd try, because by this time I had become much more proficient in the art of picking up blitzes. I was more experienced, obviously, and I'd learned a new technique from John Sandusky, just a matter of which foot to move first.

"That day Nitschke blitzed 75 percent of the plays. It started with the first play of the game and it went on *all* the way through. He never touched nor came within five yards of the quarterback. It was one of the most satisfying games of my whole career. All of this sounds so vindictive . . . which it is. It was quite simply a case where I took tremendous pleasure in using just every *ounce* to smash him with, because of all the humiliation he had caused me.

"Then, the last time I saw him was when I was with the Oilers and we went to Milwaukee to play the Packers in our third exhibition game. I walked into the lobby of the Pfister Hotel back there and it was as if I'd walked through a time warp. I looked over and there was Nitschke. It was eerie. He seemed such a genuine anachronism . . . and I don't mean that in an unkind way, but like a sultan, or some potentate of ancient times . . . this regal presence that Ray Nitschke has. There he sat, with his gleaming dome, surveying, as I say, what had been *his* for many years. He was trying to struggle back for his sixteenth year as an NFL linebacker, and from what I had heard through the grapevine, he was not being successful. I felt very awkward trying to speak to this man who had broken me into the NFL in such a rigorous fashion. The conversation went something like this: 'Gee, Ray, how are you? How's Jackie? How're the kids?' 'Oh, Bill, they're fine. We just got a little girl. . . .' They have, I think, three children now. Then there was an awkward pause, and he suddenly blurted out: 'Bill, I can play. I can go. I can do it.' And I said, 'Well, I heard you were going to get to play tonight.' He said, 'I don't know about that, but I can go.' He looked at me and he said, 'If I do get to play, you better buckle it up.' I said, 'Well, I've always had to buckle it up against you.' He said, 'Yeah, but I'm fighting for my life this time.'

"That night it was worse. The game was bad, as usual. We got behind by 17 to nothing in just a matter of half a quarter; we came surging back and made it 17 to 14, and then we went on to lose the game about 34 to 14, something like that. Suddenly, with about five minutes left, these fifty thousand people in County Stadium began to chant: *'We want Nitschke, We want Nitschke, We want Nitschke.'* In Milwaukee the benches are arranged so that both of them are on the same side of the field. I had been taken out of the game, through for the night, and so I just walked down to the far end to be near the Packer players. I stood there watching Ray. He didn't move. It was as if he were a statue. It was as if the Divine were trying to make His statue of him before he wanted to be one. In fact, it reminded me of Dan Sullivan's great line about John Unitas: 'Unitas is the only guy whose number they tried to retire while he was still in the jersey.' That was what was happening to Ray, and it was very sad. They never did put him in the game.

"After the game I ran over and grabbed him by the arm and talked with him for a minute. He told me that Hog Hanner, who's one of the coaches at Green Bay and who played there for many years with Ray before coaching, had said, 'Well, I hope we can get you in. They love you here.' Ray thought that was strange, kind of funny.

"Then I took the hand of this man who had humiliated me and castigated me, stomped me physically and emotionally during my first two years with the Packers, and I said, 'Ray, I've never thanked you for what you did for me.' I meant it sincerely because he helped to make me a lot tougher than I'd ever been before. In Ray's own, very unique way, he meant it as an effort to help me improve; certainly wasn't a pleasant way to do it, but I think he knew that . . . and I said, 'Ray, I've never thanked you.' He said, 'Yes, you have, you've thanked me. There're a lot of ways of saying thanks besides verbally.'

"I watched him run off County Stadium's field for the last time. That big 66 and that unique gait he has, leaning forward, huge shoulders and arms pumping slightly, skinny calves. I realized that I had just touched a legend, and was seeing him brought down by the very sport that he had helped build. The same way I've seen John Unitas and Tom Matte and others.

"I guess that's the way life is. Players have such a limited amount of time—though of course they think their careers are going to go on forever. Most of them don't prepare for the day it stops. They don't take off-season jobs. Their excuse is, 'Well, there's always July. . . .' Another training season is rolling around—one more July—and everything will be as it always was."

Chapter 16

"Look, there's a sign," Curry exclaimed. "FOND DU LAC 17, GREEN BAY 89. Whew! It's enough to get the butterflies sailing around."

I could hear him draw in his breath. "Fond du Lac," he said, picking the less pertinent town, perhaps to get his mind off football. "You begin to get a lot of French names up here— French explorers like Marquette came through. Did I ever tell you about the football game an NFL group played in Paris?"

"You're kidding," I said.

"It was put together by a friend who's just over on the other side of the insanity line. His name is Bubba Sutton . . . a Marietta, Georgia, boy who has the eerie talent of organizing almost anything in almost no time, and he gets it together *enough* so that it's just barely hanging together with bubble gum. He's always dragging me into his stupid projects, and I'm always stupid enough to go along with them. Bubba got the crazy idea to take a bunch of NFL football players to Paris and play an

177

exhibition game. He thought the French would flock to see it. He thought the promotion might make scads of money.

"The first thing Bubba did was to quit his job as a vice-president for a New York advertising agency and buy himself a plane ticket to Paris, where he started wandering around the American community asking questions. He just knocks on people's doors. That's how he got Bob Hope to go with us. He knocked on his door. He's like Billy Rose in *Funny Lady*. If he wants to get somebody to do something, all he has to do is get in front of him. . . . The person has almost *no* chance of getting out of it, no matter how ludicrous the idea is. He doesn't look as though he could pull much weight . . . totally bald except for some long, stringy hair hanging down the back. He used to wear horn-rimmed glasses, though now he wears little wire specs to make him look mod. He's pale and sort of frail-looking. Not prepossessing. But he's very charming, witty; he can charm anybody. In Paris he got to know E. Ernest Goldstein, who was a legal adviser of former President Lyndon Johnson and a prominent attorney in Paris. He got in to see Ambassador Watson, former chairman of the board of IBM. He involved him. Through Tom Matte he got Vice-President Spiro Agnew to be an honorary chairman. Poor Tom; I don't think he knew what he was getting into either.

"Then Bubba came back and started dickering around with Pan American Airlines. He had all these balls up in the air, though nothing had actually happened—everything was kind of floating. He showed up at our players' representatives meeting in 1972 in Key Biscayne, Florida. I said, 'Bubba, don't you dare say anything to those reps about Paris plans that you can't deliver. Tell them exactly the way everything stands. Don't get them excited about something that you can't do.' He said, 'Bill, I promise you I'm not going to. I'm just going to discuss the idea and see if I can't get some guys to help me on some of this . . . you know, help raise some money, and talk about how much fun it would be. That's all I'm going to do, I promise.' I said,

'Okay, fine.' So we gave him a spot on the agenda to discuss the *possibilities* of going over there.

"At the meeting he walked in and said, 'Gentlemen, I'd like to invite you and your wives to a company meeting in Paris, France, as the guests of Ambassador Watson, E. Ernest Goldstein . . .' I wanted to choke him; I wanted to kill him. He got 'em all fired up; we had our wives with us down there and you can imagine what the news did to them. Naturally, the place just went sky high.

"I found out later that he didn't have *anything* done at this point. I asked, 'Do you mean you didn't have any idea of how you were going to get us *over* there, or where we were going to stay, or where we were going to play?' He said, 'Nothing. Nothing.'

"This was in February. By May, forty players and their wives went to Paris, all complimentary. In the interim Bubba had some interesting experiences, during which he almost lost his mind, and he *did* end up bankrupt, but he got us over there. Bob Hope did a stand-up hour show for us at a black-tie affair at a fabulous old theater there, along with Benny Goodman, and I don't know how the hell Bubba got Hope *or* Goodman. We had a golf tournament, which Billy Casper came over to handle for us. We had a great cocktail party on the Île St. Louis, in a fantastic apartment. I was standing there talking with this character who had on a safari jacket. We were both feeling pretty good and staring out over the Seine, when somebody came up and said, 'Mr. Jones, how are you? I just thought your last book was terrific.' It was James Jones of *From Here to Eternity* standing there! I'd been talking to him for a half hour. Bubba had put all this together.

"By and large we had a terrific time. Of course, there were some problems. There was a bus strike going on and we couldn't get to a lot of our functions. People got upset and I was the guy whose phone always rang at two in the morning if somebody had been stranded somewhere. 'Hey, Curry?' 'What it is brother man?' 'How am I going to get back to the hotel?' 'Gosh, I don't know. I don't even know where you are.' 'Gyat-da*ham*, man. How come this bus ain't come to pick us up?' 'I don't know. I guess they're on strike.' Well, you know how tours are."

"Yes," I said. "The idea of Bob Hayes standing around the Trocadero waiting for a bus."

"Exactly. We just went on having a good time until it came down to the football game. Of course, we couldn't play a real football game. Our insurance could not apply to a real contact-type game. But Bubba in his incredible way had promised that we *would* and he got the French excited enough to get it on national French television.

"I guess it looked a *little* like a football game. Two French Rugby teams had played a match just prior to ours. Then we went out—a blue team and a red team. Because of the Olympics, Bob Hayes—who had won gold medals in the dashes—was really quite the toast of Paris while we were there—'Le Bub' Hayes. So we had Pastorini throw Le Bub Hayes a couple of seventy-yarders for touchdowns, and they cheered. We had about twelve thousand people there, which was capacity for the stadium. It was a good crowd. The ambassador was there.

"It was all programmed, of course. The quarterback would come to the line of scrimmage and call out so everybody on both sides of the line could hear, 'Sweep right for eight yards.' So Tom Matte or someone would be assigned to run eight yards and then somebody's come up and knock him down. Then the quarterback'd come up to the line and he'd call out, 'Sweep left for a touchdown.'

"Jim Kiick, who was then playing for the Dolphins, was the one who was supposed to run for a touchdown. When the play started, I fired out on Willie Lanier and as I hit him he fell down and I fell on top of him. We lay there a minute. He lifted his head and kind of looked around to see what was happening. I asked, 'Has Kiick come by here?' He said, 'No; we'd better stay down here a minute.' It seemed like about ten seconds had passed. I said, 'Where the hell is Kiick?' About this time Kiick finally came running by us, people diving on the ground and missing him, and since he was tired out and looked like he was about to fall down himself, they were calling to him, 'Don't fall down, Kiick, you've got to go all the way!' So he kept dodging tacklers. A really great-looking run. He finally got into the end zone, but what had made it such a long run was that he had fumbled the hand-off; it had taken him about fifteen seconds to pick it up back there. In my case, it goes down in history as my greatest block on Willie Lanier. Might be the only time I *ever* blocked him!

"The huddles were a riot. I wish I could remember . . . people laughing at each other so they could barely stand up. Big Ben Davidson got up a terrific act for the opening kickoff. He was the wedge-buster and he came running down, just *flying* down. Tom Keating was to block on him, and they'd worked it out so that when Tom hit him below the knees, Big Ben would do these three great flips in the air and land on his head. The two could handle it because they're both in such great physical shape. Of course, the place went crazy when they did it.

"We had a couple of quarterback sacks to excite them, too. We told Pastorini when they were coming. 'Hey, you're going to get sacked this time.' He said, 'Thanks a lot, fellows.' So Rick Redman of the Cards blitzed and I let him go by. Pastorini started shuffling back with the ball and Redman was in such poor shape that he almost ran out of gas before he got back there to tackle him.

"We had one anxious moment. We'd assigned 'Le Bub' Hayes to run a reverse, and Alan Page forgot where he was. As Hayes cut back, Page *really* cut him down. Hayes was upset. He asked, 'What are you doing?' Alan said, 'I don't know, man. I forgot! I'm sorry. You were just there, I just didn't . . .'

"Then this strange thing happened right at the end of the game. John Bragg was our referee, the representative with Adidas shoes, who actually provided us with the most enjoyable thing we did—a dinner on the Seine one night with wine. It was great. Dr. Cary Middlecoff, the golfer, was with us. I don't know how Bubba got these people, but he got them. Anyhow, John was our referee. A time-out was called and an official came over and told him something. He got this funny look on his face. So I walked over. He said to me, 'Run out there to the huddle and tell them not to go to the locker room at the end of the game.' I said, 'What are you talking about? All our valuables and our clothes and stuff are in there.' 'Yeah, but we've had a bomb threat.' So I went running out to the huddle, where everybody was rocking back and forth laughing, wondering what sort of play to come up with next, and I leaned in and said, 'Fellows, guess what? There's a bomb in our locker room. Don't go in there.' That must have been a first for a huddle. We went to the line of scrimmage and Pastorini, standing under the center, announced across to the defense, 'Hey, everybody, there's a bomb in the locker room. Don't be goin' in there after the game!'

"Maybe the bomb threat came from a disgruntled Frenchman. Because the next day the reviews of our performance came out. I think *L'Équipe* was the most scathing. The lead read: 'Relax, Frenchmen, our national game is in no jeopardy.' No one seemed to accept that it was an exhibition. One of the other papers said: 'The American game is static, lacking in imagination, and the players are clearly in precarious physical condition.' Well, *that* was true. We had a bunch of fat guys out there. It was early in May and nobody was in shape. I'm sure all of us had a little tub hanging out. Seems to me that Dave Costa was rather round; Rich Jackson was pretty hefty; Merlin was very large. The biggest laugh of the day was when the defensive linemen were warming up and doing carioca drills back and forth across the field. The Frenchmen just couldn't believe their *eyes*. Here were these behemoths with these bouncing bellies doing this ballet dance, the carioca—that shuttling little crablike sideways drill that linemen do by crisscrossing their feet. There were just peals of laughter coming out of the stands.

"It was fun. We were there in Paris four or five days. Absolutely no practice sessions. We had one walk-through at the hotel in the ballroom, where we told everybody what position they were going to play. The whole thing was hilarious. You know how Rugby players swap jerseys at the end of the game? Well, the French Rugby guys came out at the end and we swapped jerseys. It was warm. It was nice."

Chapter 17

Curry pointed out the window. "See the statues there on the lawn—those two blackamoor stableboys with their hands out? Hitching posts. Boy, you don't see those in the South anymore. We had a neighbor who had a pair. They put them out behind the barn . . . and then they disappeared altogether."

We drove on for a while. Curry said, "I really am beginning to get those butterflies, I swear, really building. I wonder who they'll have me rooming with up there."

"Do you have any choice?" I asked.

"With the Packers you were told who you roomed with. At the Packers you were told everything."

Curry asked me what sort of roommates I'd had in college—were they athletes?—and I said, Goodness, no . . . not at all. There were three of us. But we went to the games at the Harvard stadium together and supported the team very vociferously. One of them, Farwell Smith, who now works in Washington as an environmentalist, always spent the game threatening to get on the field and "help" the football team. He wanted to "fill in," as he put it, as an extra tackle. The reason he never did was that he was hampered by a twisted trombone he carried at games (it looked as if it had been run over by a car), out of which he managed to produce a bray of sorts, very loud. It kept coming apart in his hands, and putting it back together occupied him.

Curry grunted slightly and asked about the other roommate.

"Well, he was a Bostonian—still lives there—Josiah Child," I told him, "and at that time he had all sorts of pretensions to being, well, *famous*, and beloved by great throngs, like an emporer, or Gandhi, and he went to football games, among other reasons, so that he could practice acknowledging cheers. When Harvard did something extraordinary—say, made a first down (we had very poor teams in those days)—he would rise slowly to his feet and accept the cheering as if it were for *him*, raising his arms and waving them about in a very lordly manner, bathing in the cheers, sometimes turning to face the yelling people up in the stands behind us, a wide politician's smile set for imaginary cameras. He was difficult to explain."

"I should say so," Curry said. "And so is that guy with the bent trombone."

"Yes. I remember that when Smith was struggling to put the thing together, he'd shout at me, 'Go on out there for me. Take my place. The team *needs* you!' "

I explained that Harvard football had traditionally been identified by a twist of irreverence—such cheers as "Fight fiercely!" rose out of the stands, or lovely French-horn choruses from Vivaldi, and there was one cheer in my day with a woodwind accompaniment in which we were supposed to shout, "Pshaw! Pshaw!" In this sort of environment, supporters such as Smith and Child were not the exception.

"Pshaw? Pshaw?" repeated Curry.

"Pshaw. The *P* is almost silent. It was used when something discouraging happened to Harvard, such as a missed field goal from the eight-yard line, and that strange sibilant cheer would drift out of the stands like a type of keening."

I told Curry about one game in which the crowd's attention —which had been flagging—was attracted by the performance of a pigeon which landed on the Harvard four-yard line, turning as soon as he put down and setting out toward the goal line with great determination, his neck bobbing in his haste. But then indecision, or something startling in the grass, diverted his attention, and he stopped a foot or two short. He revolved peering here and there . . . and suddenly that immense crowd focused on him, neighbors nudging each other and remarking on the pigeon's vacillation just at the brink of the goal line. Megaphones went up; cries of "Go, bird, go!" erupted from one side of the stadium, and "Hold that pigeon!" from the Harvard side.

As I recall, he crossed the line. The stands across the way were exultant. On our side, gloom. The woodwinds struck up and we called out, "Pshaw! Pshaw!"

"It really hurt," Curry said.

"Oh, yes," I said.

Curry shook his head. "Frankly, I don't know what would have happened to my football potential in an environment like that."

"Presumably your roommates were more traditional," I suggested.

"Come to think of it," Curry replied, "I'm not so sure. But at least they were football players. . . . My first roommate my rookie year at Green Bay was Allen Brown. He was from Mississippi, and had a lot of injuries, and he ended up leaving in 1967."

"He was black?"

"Oh, no, he was white. He played at ol' Miss! In 1965, if you were from ol' Miss, there ain't but one color, brother. It was sad because he was a pretty good player, and he got bummed up in the All-Star camp and he just never did quite make it at

Green Bay, mainly, I think, because of his injuries. He and I used to wake up every morning, and we'd look at each other. The only thing he'd say was, 'Oh, me. Ohhhh, me.' That immediately put me in a good frame of mind for the day. I'd respond with 'Ohhhh, me.' That's about the extent of it. He played tight end. One funny thing he did . . . these stupid little jokes that athletes pull. He didn't usually say very much; he was quiet. One day he walked up to practice with me. Of course, Lombardi was parading around and screaming at everybody, as usual.

"Allen suddenly said, 'You know what just burns my ass?'

" 'No.'

"He held his hand down about three feet off the ground. 'A little flame about this high,' he said. Coming from him, it just broke me up. Caught me completely off guard.

"The next year at Green Bay I had Allen Jacobs. We talked about him in our composite. He's a little tough fellow that we ended up trading to the Giants. Came from Utah. Allen had his own thing going, too. One day I asked, 'What did you do in the off-season, Allen?'

" 'Well, I really had a lot of fun,' he said. 'Had a *good* off-season.'

" 'What did you do?'

" 'My wife and I have a home out in Utah now,' he said. 'I fixed up my basement real nice and I spent most of my time down there.'

" 'Oh, you've got a carpentry shop?'

" 'No, no,' he said. "I've got a Ping-Pong table down there and I just love to play. I go down there and I play all day almost every day.'

" 'Who'd you play with?' I asked.

" 'Well, I didn't have anybody to play with so I backed the table up against the wall. . . .' He was *dead serious;* he never smiled! He would stand down there and play solitaire Ping-Pong, using the wall to bounce the ball back to him. He said,

187

'Also, I had a nice television down there and I used to watch a lot of TV. I really had a *great* off-season; it was fun!' "

I remarked that I had been doing a piece for *Sports Illustrated* on what athletes did for hobbies or on their vacations in the off-season, and that certainly Jacobs was going to rank right up there with the oddest.

"I should think so," Curry said.

He wanted to know what else my research had turned up. I told him that the most surprising had been Dave Schultz's, the "hit man" on the Philadelphia Flyers hockey team, who was known as "The Hammer," for his ferocity. In the off-season, his hobby was to build radio-controlled ship models, motor launches, most of them—delicate, painstakingly put together—and when they were finished and lacquered, he took them down to the lake and lovingly put them on the water. They had little lead people on board. He sat there on a beach chair with the radio set in his lap, working the controls and watching his craft turning in big circles around the swimming float. Not quite what one would expect of "The Hammer."

"No," Curry agreed.

"But then I found out," I went on, "that occasionally he'd hide in the bushes by the water and sneak one of his boats out by the people lolling in the water by the float . . . just easing the boat up to them very quietly, working up on them from the rear, and then suddenly one of the swimmers would sense something behind him, and turn to discover Schultz's PT boat or the *Queen Elizabeth*, or whatever, just inches away, with a crowd of lead people staring at him—quite a sight at water level—and then Dave would push the throttle forward on his radio set and the boat would barrel out of there with the thin, high whine of a tiny propeller."

"Well, that sounds more like it," Curry said. "At least he doesn't run them down."

"Next summer perhaps," I said. "Bill, who was your roommate at Baltimore?"

"Mike Curtis," Curry replied. "Metal Mike, for five years. We started off calling him Iron Mike because he was so tough; and then he tore his knee up, so Don Shinnick demoted him to Metal Mike. Then, when he lost a lot of weight and came around with a cast on his leg, Shinnick scaled him down to something like Fabric Mike or Cloth Mike, Paper Mike, I think. It ended up with Shinnick calling him Air Mike the last couple of months. He had withered in the cast during that time.

"Of course, that's not an impression opposing teams had. He was a devastating player. He drove all of us. Talk about 'just football!' He'd discipline his own players; he'd kick the linemen in front of him, or shove at them to move them over, shouting at them. The one lineman he couldn't do that to was Billy Ray Smith. 'Don't you ever touch me, it distracts me,' Billy Ray said —odd to think that in a sport with so much laying on of hands you'd ever hear a football player say such a thing—and Mike Curtis always avoided him. But that didn't stop him with the rest of us. He wasn't the team captain or even the defensive captain, but in 1970 he stood up in front of the entire team and he said, 'I'll make sure that you go all out for the rest of the season because if I ever see anyone who's not giving 100 percent, I'll beat his ass.' We had three games left in the regular season, three in the playoffs, including the Super Bowl, and we won all six.

"Mike had a very firm idea that you had to do that sort of thing to make a team work. In fact, he went to Coach McCafferty when the team began to sag in 1972 and told him he wasn't handling the team properly and in essence suggested that he change his personality and start shouting at his players.

"Mac said, 'You're telling me, Mike, you want me to yell at you?'

" 'Yeah,' Mike said. 'If you think it's necessary.'

"A week later we were playing in Buffalo and Mike missed a sidelines tackle and rolled right up under Mac's feet. Mac leaned down and he asked, real quiet, 'Mike, what're you doing?'

"Mike jumped up and he said, 'I'm hustling my ass off.'

"Mac said, 'Well, then, would you hit someone when you get there, please.' "

"What sort of procedures did the two of you go through on the day of a game?" I asked.

"We'd get up and drive over to Memorial Stadium in Mike's car," Curry said. "The superloyal fans were already there—three and a half hours before game time—and they'd slap us on the back as we'd kind of strut down that ramp into the stadium. I remember the way Mike walked. I'd sign autographs, but he wanted to push on; he already had his mind on what was coming. He might perfunctorily write something that looked like 'Mike Curtis.'

"That was an important part of my own preparation—to walk into the stadium with Mike. It was almost as if I could draw on his strength. . . . Just the way he walked helped me get ready to play.

"Part of the scene in the Colt locker room was having friends down there before a game. Most coaches don't want anybody in the locker room hobnobbing around, but on Carroll Rosenbloom's team, he was always in there, and he would have some friends with him. It was part of the ritual. Joe Thomas, when he took over after Carroll sold the team, was aghast . . . people standing around and chatting. But it wasn't a big deal; it was a part of the whole Colt family thing.

"But Mike didn't like it at all; it wasn't the way he thought things should be. So he would get there very early. I might wander around talking to people; I'd look back and Mike would be completely dressed . . . taped, his pads on, shoulder pads, everything. He'd go in the training room; he'd get a radio, turn it up real loud, and sit there with his ear against it and kind of rock back and forth. He'd do that for a couple of hours. I don't know if he went over his assignments while he listened, or if he

190

just let his mind wander, or if he meditated. I never talked to him about it; but by the time we were on the field for warm-ups he was almost in a trance. He and I had a ritual that we followed precisely. We never talked about it, but we always did the same thing. At a stage in the warm-ups, we'd stand and look at each other; he would point at one shoulder and I'd come off the ball full speed and we'd smash shoulders together. He'd explode. It would rock me right down to my toes. Then he'd point at the other shoulder, and we'd hit again. That started the ignition. Then after our pregame talk in the locker room, Mike and I would find each other again. You know how you lock arms and hit your shoulders together? Well, we would hit each other with absolutely all our might, just tremendous smashes. Many times I would see stars. And I knew I was ready to play, because nobody was going to hit me any harder than Mike just had."

"Did you communicate during the game?" I asked.

"When we'd score a touchdown, I'd come off and I'd look for Mike. It was important to me that we win Mike's approval somehow. He'd look at me and he would nod. If I had made a good play—a good block on a screen pass or something—he might even say something. But never much. Mutual encouragement was involved, but without any of the back-slapping and hugging stuff that the rest of us did. Mike didn't usually engage in that sort of thing. He was apart. It was an interesting relationship. In the middle of the players' strike controversy, all of it so heated, where he and I had taken totally opposite positions, he told me he was going to break the strike and go to camp, the first veteran to do so. He really knocked our philosophical position. I called him up to ask him about some of the things he had said. We were just poles apart! But then he asked me if I could come to dinner to see their new baby."

"I remember his locker at the stadium," I said. "He had a big picture of Spiro Agnew hanging up there."

"Well, during those five years we roomed together, we differed on virtually everything of substance," Curry said. "Still, we had a good time together; we respected each other. We worked hard against each other in practice, and every now and then we'd have a little fistfight and knock each other around and I'd end up with tears in my eyes. Kind of embarrassing. Then after practice we'd laugh about it. But in 1971 things got a little tense. Mike wasn't happy with the coaching staff and especially he wasn't happy with the performance of the offense. It got tense in the room. We argued. Also, we had very different habits. He liked to sleep about fourteen hours a night. Sometimes he couldn't. He'd be over there with his eyes squinched closed and his teeth gritting, forcing himself to stay on the bed so his body could rest. I'm not exaggerating that. He was *going* to get that rest, even at his own expense. He just forced himself. If I dropped a coat hanger, or if I got up and turned on the water, he'd toss over; it bothered him. Also, he'd stuff towels around the windows to keep any light from getting in. Finally I called him in the off-season of '71 and said, 'Why don't we make things easier on ourselves? It'll probably help our relationship considerably if we don't room together.' He was relieved. He said, 'I really appreciate your calling and talking about it man to man. I agree.'

"So after that I ended up rooming with John Mackey, which was a great education. We used to lie awake for hours into the night. . . . He would try to explain to me what it had been like to grow up. In his case, he grew up on Long Island and he didn't realize what prejudice was until he drove South with his parents one time. They were traveling to South Carolina to visit relatives. In Virginia they pulled up at a place, and John thought it was a little strange that his parents didn't get out. His father's a minister, apparently quite a man. Maybe this is the way he wanted John to learn. They gave him a dollar and told him to bring out a small order. John was hungry, and he went in and sat there. A white waitress waited on a number of other customers and continued to ignore him. Finally, after he had sat there about a half hour, his parents waiting out in the parking lot, she told him that she would not be able to serve him; he had to leave. He still didn't know why. He thought maybe it was because he was a little boy. His dad began to tell him why bit by bit.

"Their relatives out in the country in South Carolina didn't have running water or plumbing or anything. He was sent to the well to get some water. As he was carrying the bucket back, a white lady came to the well. She had her bucket. He said, 'Do you want me to help you? Can I fill your bucket up for you?' She said, 'I don't need any help from a nigger.' He threw his bucket of water in her face, calmly filled it again and walked to the house, where he told his father what he had done. He was about ten or twelve. Whereupon, his father took him bodily and threw him in the car, and they drove something like twenty-four straight hours back to Long Island without ever slowing up. You can imagine what they would've done to him in those days. That was very moving for me, being from the South, and trying to think of a perfectly innocent black child being confronted with that. He didn't even know what the word *Nigger* meant at the time.

"John was a pretty realistic guy; he's not any sort of flag-waving radical at all. He realized the limitations of the Players Association, which he was president of, and I might add he realized them a good bit better than I did. John Mackey is one of the more remarkable people that I have known. What a football player! If you took the history of the NFL and picked out the twenty most exciting plays that have ever occurred, he'd probably have six of them. Those runs he used to make were just *unbelievable!* Just defy description. You'd have to see him . . . tackler after tackler after tackler falling off him. He did one against Chicago in 1968 when I was on the team. I wasn't in the game at the time. I could watch it. It was just staggering! He was running over linebackers and whirling and stomping and springing past these little fleet safety men, because he could outrun *them,* too. Rosey Taylor, who at that time was still with

193

the Bears, a real fine safety, jumped on John's back at about the fifteen-yard line, and then finally fell off at about the five because he wasn't having the slightest effect: John just trotted on into the end zone.

"He had his best games in Kezar Stadium, San Francisco. Kezar Stadium was literally a worm bed if it rained a lot, which it does all the time in San Francisco, and if it rained before the game we'd go out there and find night crawlers—just thousands of them—all over the turf. Mackey had a terrible fear of any kind of animal; he doesn't like insects either. He'd rather just stay away from them. But these worms! He just didn't want them on his body. Against San Francisco one day, John caught about six passes for 150 yards or so, and they never *got him on the ground*. He wouldn't go down. . . . He just kept those massive thighs churning, and he'd finally push himself and everybody else out of bounds and they'd have to let him go. He had one of the great games of his career because of those worms.

"We used to do terrible things to Mackey. Dennis Gaubatz, one of our linebackers, put a snake in his shirt one day at training camp in Maryland. The snake was dead. It was funny because when Mackey pulled the shirt out of his locker he was looking the other way. Everybody in the locker room was giggling. The snake fell down in his shoes. Then after he had put his shirt on, he sat down to pick up his shoes, and of course his legs were so powerful that when he saw the snake he just sprang out of his seat for about ten feet across the floor. Another time at training camp Gaubatz put a live possum in his locker. The locker room opened onto a hallway. Girls walked around there, which meant you had to be dressed, at least with a towel around your waist, to walk around outside. I was upstairs, and when I came down the stairs from getting my ankles taped, I saw Mackey standing in the middle of that hallway buck naked. Absolutely not a stitch of clothes! I asked, 'John, what's wrong?' He was shaking. He said, 'There's something in my locker! And it's breathing!' I said, 'What is it?' He said, 'I don't know, man. Would you go get it?' I said, 'Get out of the hallway; you're naked.' He said, 'I don't care. I'm not going back in that room till you get that thing out of my locker!'

"We had to get Gaubatz to get that possum out. I didn't want to reach in there either; a possum'll bite you.

"Another thing they did to Mackey. Every now and then in Westminster where we trained there'd be a tremendous influx of locusts . . . hanging off the trees and making those whirring noises. Great big insects. Somebody took one of them alive and put it inside Mackey's football pants. We'd wear pants out to practice without thigh pads, so they put the locust in the pocket that would have ordinarily been used for the pad. We started out to practice and, strangely enough, the creature was quiet. Naturally, everybody was standing around anticipating. Nothing happened! We had our short meeting, went down on the field, and we started in on team plays. We were standing in the huddle and all of a sudden there was this *kkkkkch*. Nobody said anything, everybody with their heads down trying to keep from laughing. Then we heard it again: *Kkkkkch*. Mackey says, 'What's that?' Nobody said anything. *Kkkkkkch*. Suddenly he realized that the sound was coming from very close by, and he reached down and felt that locust in his britches. Well, he stripped his pants off—I'm not exaggerating—he came out of those pants in a matter of just a split second or so. He didn't bother to untie them or unzip them or anything. Just ripped 'em off! Right there in the huddle. He wouldn't wear them again until we got that dadgummed thing out and set it free.

"At Houston it was a complete turnaround from the sort of time I'd had with Mackey. I was put with Dan Pastorini, the Oiler quarterback. It made sense. I was supposed to be a stabilizing influence on this young, highly talented player with vast potential and a hot temper. He had taken a terrible beating the previous two years, and that takes a toll. He could have been a linebacker, the way he was involved with collision. We talked about it in the evenings—quite a complex social and psychological matter to deal with: how you handle this sort of situation, how you relate to your teammates when you know they're not doing a good job, and they know it, too, and they're feeling a little guilty. We talked around the clock. We rode around Texas in his little De Tomaso Pantera, which was orange, and we went 140 mph, and we wore cowboy boots. We bought ourselves harmonicas and tried to play duets—silly things—but always our minds came back to his problems as a quarterback and how to resolve them. He was very determined. He had all these workout gimmicks on which he would train in the room— which helped him to be remarkably conditioned. Those things really cluttered up our room."

I asked what sort of interior decorating went on in training camp.

"Usually there's very little decoration," Curry said. "I remember Billy Ray Smith had stock charts around his room . . . but that was because he was very serious about the market and knew he was going into the brokerage business when he was finally through with football. Black guys always had their picks lying around—those big wide-spaced combs for their 'naturals.' Always a larger emphasis on music. Bubba Smith had music on all the time. Sometimes we got things from fans. There was a wonderful wacky pair of girls from Hartford, Connecticut, who called themselves 'Mischief Control'—the most rabid Baltimore Colt fans. They knitted mats with knobbly things that felt funny under the toes for us to stand on in front of our lockers. They sent one to me. Bubba Smith stood on it one day, a smile crossed his face, and then he appropriated it to put in front of *his* locker. But there is quite a variance of what athletes bring to training. You can see how much junk I have in the back seat. Mike Curtis came with nothing, a little bag with two pairs of Levi's in there, a rubber-thonged pair of sandals, and a Duke Blue Devil T-shirt. He didn't even bring shorts, since the Colts would provide those. He had a cowboy hat. I pitched in with a record player, a TV, a radio, and one year I got him to share the expense of an air-conditioner. When we broke camp, it seems to me he ended up with it. One July I arrived with perhaps three shirts and a couple of pairs of trousers and Mike sat on the bed and looked at me aghast. 'Oh, my God,' he said. 'You've turned into a clotheshorse.' That was Mike. Pastorini, on the other hand, arrived with enough shirts to fill the most demanding of social calendars: he was *ready*. His Levi's were decorated with all these clever little designs and patches that his wife, June, sewed on—one of them, as I remember, a phrase on his left buttock that read 'Kiss My Patch.' That sort of thing."

I asked Curry if he thought there would be the usual training-camp high jinks up at Green Bay.

"Oh, sure," he said. "Even there. There's a sort of juvenile attitude hits us in July. No matter how mature the guys are, it's very easy to get a sort of dormitory attitude at training camp. After all, it's the same routine that exists in school . . . you go to classes, drill period, athletics, and then a monitor comes around at lights out and makes sure you're in bed. Just as kids bridle at this sort of authority, with the football players a sort of kid mentality begins to take over . . . a reversion to wacky behavior. It consumes even the unsuspecting types—with the Colts, people like Earl Morrall and John Unitas, who roomed together . . . very contagious . . . and then when camp was about to break, just about everybody'd go berserk. Ted Hendricks, the Mad Stork, went crazy with a fire extinguisher one year, about three in the morning, and water fights broke out up and down the landings and corridors of the dormitory . . . everyone giggling and carrying on like crazy kids. Then word came that Coach McCafferty was on his way, which meant big fines were going to be handed out. Everybody sprinted for his room . . . but neither Morrall nor Dan Sullivan could make it. They ducked into the bathroom. Sully was buck naked so he just sat down on the john. McCafferty stuck his head in and said, 'Hello, Sully.' And Sully said, 'Hello, Coach.' But the shower was running and it was three o'clock in the morning. So McCafferty went over and snatched the shower curtain back and there was Earl standing there, with a little grin on his face, the water pouring down, and he was completely clothed. Even had his jacket on."

"Look there," Curry said. "Another Green Bay sign. We're moving in on the place. I guess they've already assigned me someone. Well, I'll tell you one thing—they couldn't find me a stranger roommate than the one I had at Los Angeles. He was Hacksaw Reynolds, who played middle linebacker. Jack Reynolds is his real name, and he went to the University of Tennessee. He is the epitome of the totally dedicated football player. When I came in to go to bed in the motel in Denver on the night before our first game, he had a pad on his left upper arm and he was working vigorously with it, hanging on it and testing it to see if it covered a bruise properly. He was already in bed, but here he was testing his padding to see if it was sufficient. He asked my opinion. We got it all fixed up and I think he slept with it on."

"I remember stories about him," I said. "Fred Dryer of the Rams once told me that he had this strange physical camaraderie with his brother. When they were kids, the two of them would climb into the inner tube of an earth-moving-machine tire, a huge discarded one they had found on some trash heap somewhere, and they'd roll down the Tennessee hills in that thing, just bowling right through the vegetable plots, lean-tos, and shanties, and about anything else in their way."

"That sounds like him."

"He once told Dryer that the two of them had a game in which one brother would climb up to the top of a tree and the other would cut it down. They both got a great kick out of that."

"Yes," Curry said. "I've heard the one about the tree."

"Tell about his nickname."

"Yes," Curry said. "Hacksaw. Well, when I asked him, he answered me quite nonchalantly. 'I sawed a car in half,' he said, as if to say: How do you *think* I got it?

" 'You what! You sawed a car in half?'

"He said, 'Yeah. I really got upset after Ol' Miss beat us 31 to nothing in my junior year. So I went out to the junkyard and I sawed a car in half.'

" 'How did you go about doing that?'

" 'How the hell do you think?' he said. 'You *saw* it! You get a hacksaw and you saw the car in half.'

" 'How long did it take you?' I asked.

" 'Two days.'

" 'Well, what did you use?' I asked.

" 'I told you!' he said. 'I used a hacksaw.'

" 'How long?' He held up his hands, indicating a typical little eight-inch blade. He said, 'There's only one kind of hacksaw and that's what I used. I sawed through the axles and the chassis and the roof and the floor and everything. I got it completely in half. What really *pissed* me off was that somebody came and stole both halves of the car.'

" 'You were going to keep it?'

" 'Sure, why do you think I did it?' "

Chapter 18

The closer we got to Green Bay, the more I could feel the tension rise in Curry—long periods of silence, the radio murmuring, and then abruptly he would speak: "I keep thinking we should have gone left on Route 33 way back there. Have you seen any signs? Seems to me that they kept them *painted* better when I was through here before . . . Wisconsin! Look how neat those fields are. . . . We get such a bad reputation in the South —Georgia—where you ride along past those broken-down ramshackle places. . . ."

Finally I interrupted: "Bill, I would think it would be the most predictable thing up there. There's nothing that's going to surprise you. Isn't every training camp just like every other? In fact, I should think you'd go bonkers with the boredom of it."

"Except that you don't know how you're going to perform, you're right," Curry said. "Everything else is predictable. The color of the helmets will be different, the personnel . . . but the daily schedules will be the same. The classes. Even what's said in the classes. It's all utterly familiar. I've sat through so many classes that there's *no way* that I can make myself listen."

"That'll be your big worry—to keep from going crazy with boredom," I said.

"There are a number of things you can do to keep from going bonkers," Curry said. "Especially if, like on the Colts, you can find a Danny Sullivan to sit back there and . . . pass gas. Of his own volition. One of the most amazing abilities. He had this odd habit of describing what he'd just done. He'd burp and then say, 'That's a burp.' So he'd sit there and suddenly he'd say, 'That's a faht'—because he came from Boston—and a panic would go through the rear of the room. Don McCafferty would start lighting matches and throwing them in Sully's sweat suit. Sully's sweats always had dark burns over the lap because of Mac throwing matches during film sessions. If you could find diversions like that, you could survive. The most boring lecturer in the history of football, though he was a fine coach and a good friend, was Dick Bielski of the Colts when he was going over pass patterns. Lord knows, nobody on the offensive line cared where Ray Perkins or John Mackey was going to run on a 68 pass pattern. But because the coaches thought we needed general knowledge, they'd make us sit in those meetings and listen to Bielski describe the pass routes. He could talk for fifteen minutes with no trouble at all about a ten-yard hookup where the guy runs down and plants his right foot, turns to the inside, and catches the ball. I learned to snore very loud, without anybody being able to tell where it was coming from. I'd just sit perfectly motionless and take notes and everything, and all the time I'd be going z-z-z-z-z-z. Bielski'd hear this and start to look around the back of the room. I'd be looking right at him, and going z-z-z-z-z-z! But he couldn't tell. Everybody was sitting there with their heads up. I'd do that for about ten minutes, till finally Bielski'd say, 'Get those offensive linemen outta this room.' They knew it was one of us, but they couldn't figure out how we were doing it.

"Also we'd get hold of Bielski's projector. He'd lose his temper about three times a year because we would tape up his lens. Just a tiny speck of tape will work so that when he started the film there was nothing but black. There're about three different ways you could do it, so sometimes it'd take him five minutes or so to find out what we had done. Or sometimes we'd just take the whole lens out and hide it somewhere. He'd walk in: 'All right, where's the damn lens? Vogel, you jerk!' "

"I don't suppose you could fool around with Lombardi that way," I said.

"Oh, no." Curry shook his head. I don't think the thought would've ever crossed anybody's mind to fall asleep. The only disturbance I can remember was during my rookie year. I was sitting in the back of the room leaning against the wall . . . they had these chairs hooked together—I was sitting in a threesome by myself. The back legs suddenly slid out from under me. *Bam*, I hit the floor. It was right in the middle of Lombardi's lecture. It was Vince himself. I got up, boy! I shot up. I swear, if I'd shattered the first through the eighth vertebrae, I would've got up. Everybody laughed. He said, 'Are you all right?' I said something clever—I was trying to impress him. I don't know how this sort of stuff pops out of my mouth. I said, 'Only my pride is hurt.' He was supposed to smile or something. He gave me another one of those withering stares. Absolutely none of that went on with Lombardi.

"Hey, look," he called out. "We're coming up on the De Pere exit. We're here." He took the Volvo down the ramp. We stopped at a light and he cranked down the window on his side. "It's going to be the same," he said. "Just like I went through a time machine. Hell, the country *smell*—it brings it all back. . . ."

I said, "Bill, I'm just going to keep the tape recorder on, and maybe you can describe what we see here in Green Bay . . . sort of like the Stage Manager in *Our Town.*"

"Sure. We'll go over and see St. Norbert College and take a

look. I'll show you where Lombardi used to stand at night, so if anybody tried to sneak out of the dorm, there he was just standing there waiting for him. The assistant coaches would check the rooms, but after that, he would stand outside and sort of watch, you could see him standing among the trees. There's the sign: ST. NORBERT COLLEGE. Now I *really* am getting a funny feeling. I was a full-time student here one entire quarter; I studied epistemology, I studied the 'Philosophy of Man.' Being St. Norbert, naturally most of what we got was Aquinas. Also, I took a sociology course, 'Sociology in the Family.' Very good; it was accepted at full credit by my Methodist theology school.

"There's Sensenbrenner Hall, just off to the right. I guess that's where I'll be staying. I know it's where we used to live. See that big tree there? *That's* where Lombardi'd be standing about midnight. There's the dining hall over there. If you'll look carefully through those large window panes—on the far side is where I used to have to stand up in a chair and sing songs for the veterans. I *am* beginning to feel like the Stage Manager.

"That ancient yellow bus there in the lot is what we ride to practice in . . . to Green Bay, which is about six miles away. Practice was over at five, and I always came right back in the yellow bus. The veteran players disappeared right after the afternoon practice, going off in their cars, and I couldn't figure out where they were. They'd show up for dinner, and they were all in a very good mood, laughing a lot. That's how naïve I was. I was really stupid! Every now and then Tommy Joe Crutcher would say—he called me Dapper Dan—'Dapper? Why'n't you go have a barley pop with us?'

" 'A barley pop?' I said.

" 'Yeah! C'mon,' he said. 'I'll buy you a barley pop.'

"I didn't know what that was, but it sounded ominous so I didn't go.

"Dapper Dan. That's who I was. Crutcher made up nicknames for everybody. Several of the players on the Packers were assigned names out of Our Gang. Jerry Kramer was called

Spanky. Tommy Joe himself was Alfalfa. Much to his dismay, Junior Coffey became Buckwheat. He didn't think that was funny *at all*. But I did. I thought it was very funny. Paul Hornung was Goat Shoulders . . . also Trophy Head because of his huge mane; he had hair about the length we wears ours now, which of course then was very long, and no, Lombardi didn't like it. He'd come in and say, 'Paul, get it cut.' Paul'd say okay, okay, and he'd go get a haircut. I don't remember a nickname for Starr. Oh, yes: Bert, we called him—Bert Stir. Kenny Bowman was called Sam. I never knew why he was called Sam, but he was. Willie Davis was called Feelgood. As I told you: Doctah Feelgood! 'How ya feel, Willie?' 'Feel *good*, man! Feel good!" He had a way of *making* you feel good. Ron Kostelnik was called Quasimodo. Big, fat Japanese tackle. Then they called Henry Jordan Henri Jourdan, a French tackle. So we had an international set of defensive tackles. Lionel Aldridge was called The Big Train. I think Leroy Caffey was called The Big Turkey; I'm not sure why . . . . Nitschke was The Bald Eagle. . . .

"Now, this is the road we took the bus down every day.

Green Bay's a pretty little town, and it doesn't seem to have changed much at all. There's nothing else in sports like what the Packer thing means to this community. A town this size counts so much on that for its identity. What a love affair goes on between the town and the team! Fifty thousand people turn up to see the intra-squad scrimmages. At Baltimore they couldn't get ten thousand out to watch the Colts play the Dallas Cowboys. But here it's always been that way: people on vacation make Green Bay a stop on their trip . . . *just* to have come and watched the Packers practice! Of course, Lombardi used to put on a show for them. He knew what he was doing. He would always say to us, 'I don't like all these people around here,' but he never made them leave. He would say, 'It cramps my style.' Everybody'd snicker. It didn't cramp him at all! Four-letter words steaming out with the girls standing there! It couldn't've been very pleasant for the wives to watch, but they didn't come very much. Why would they want to watch us run around anyhow?

"Look at this town. It comes back not as a concept or a memory, but as an emotion; the feeling of tension comes back. The feelings reemerge almost identical to the way I felt before. Strange, when I came here as a Baltimore Colt I didn't feel that at all. I had on a different-colored shirt. I wasn't a Packer. . . . Look at that little park! Neat as a pin—every post in it painted a bright orange. They could have filmed *The Music Man* in there. It'll be a nice place to run in. I can always feel the knee, but I know how to deal with it. That hamstring, though. Just a slight tear. . . . but there is no control involved . . . so little I can do about it except wait and hope there's enough time. The doctors will help. What a coincidence!

Right up there is the Packer team doctor's office—Brusky X-Ray Clinic. See it? Dr. Brusky is the doctor. He's one doctor, and Dr. Nellin is the other.

"Max McGee and Paul Hornung used to live in one of these motels around here somewhere. I don't know which one. Paul used to tell me that he never paid any rent because every year he won it off the landlord in a gin game.

"Imagine what those houses with the little stoops out in front are like in winter. The wind blows all summer and then suddenly, about August 15, it brings in the winter. The people were friendly, in the Southern tradition, certainly. They're polite. It's just different. Of course, being Packers, we had an advantage. But I don't think we were invited anywhere or did much at all outside the football team community. I got homesick for the first couple of weeks when Carolyn wasn't with me. I just was morose. I began to get the sense of what Carolyn meant to me in terms of stability through the years. Just tremendous strength. She liked it; she likes it anywhere. As long as she's got a good book and a good school, and the children have a good school, she's happy . . . if you don't make her stay out in the cold for too long.

"We didn't *do* anything; we were home every night. We were just young little kids. If we did anything, we went to the show. Down there on the right is the Vic Theater, which Carolyn would bring me to when I was in a virtual state of immobility emotionally. There's the Bay Theater. Spent a lot of time in that one, too.

"Railroad track right up here on the right.

"There's the bay. That damn thing opposite is a big coal-loading station. Pretty bleak thing to look out on. When it's about twenty below zero and the wind's whipping across here, this is a bleak place, period!

"If you look over there you'll see Prange's Parking Lot. When we were here before, some lady backed right out of it, into the river, and drowned.

"Here's the West Theater. This is where I came to see *The Sound of Music.* I saw *Zhivago* for the third time. But it was at the Vic Theater I saw one of the movies I enjoyed as much as any movie I've ever seen. It was called *The Naked Prey.* Cornel Wilde was in it. He was the guide on a safari. They ran across this tribe which a guy who was a member of the party offended by . . . well, the tribe was hinting around that they should get some trinkets, and he told them to get lost. Cornel Wilde said, 'You shouldn'ta done that. These people are a little unpredictable.' The guy just blustered on; he said he didn't care. That night the tribe came back and captured everybody and they took them to their village, where they proceeded to systematically kill each member of the expedition in a different and more horrible fashion, one after the other. It was extremely well done! Then they took Cornel Wilde—he was the last one—and they stripped him naked, and took him out to the edge of the village and shot an arrow into the air as far as the bow would sling it, and motioned for him to start running. When he got to the arrow, they sent one guy after him. When he ran a little farther, they sent another. And another. The bulk of the movie was his experience dashing through woods and the way that he avoided their efforts to get him: he set the jungle on fire once or twice. He almost died of starvation. A snake came climbing out of a skull; he grabbed the snake and ripped his head off and ate the darned thing right there on the spot. Peeled that son-of-a-gun like a banana! Everybody in the theater gagged. He went on and he finally escaped in the end. That was my second year with the Packers, and I sat there watching that movie, thinking: Boy, this is a lot like what *I'm* doing! Those people were after me!

"We'll head out for the practice field. They'll be out there. See that drawbridge? Once when I was on this street, it was up —a tugboat and a barge going under it—and I sat there in my car, not a thing I could do, knowing that the time was creeping by and I was going to be late for Lombardi's practice. I pounded on the wheel. I blew the horn. I didn't cuss at that time but I probably tried. What could the skipper of that boat have thought? My shirt was soaked with sweat. I just made it in time. I still dream about it—the lift of the drawbridge and the funnel of the tugboat barely inching along.

"I think we take a left here on Morris Avenue. Lombardi Avenue is right up there. I'm going to show you our first apartment right by the football practice field, which we called The Closet . . . assuming that it's still there. It was not the best-constructed thing in town. Oh, look, there's a public park. The kids will like that when Carolyn arrives with them. We'll drive right down here to Oneida Street. Pretty much the same. I sure can feel the same old butterflies I felt riding on that bus down through here. Here I am again in the same place. It's weird. It's all so jumbled. I feel old and new at the same time. It's still there! Look, it's still there. We lived in the upper left corner. The building was new at the time. Carolyn could sit and look out the window and watch practice.

"Before we go out to the field we ought to duck in here and take a look at the Green Bay Packer Hall of Fame. We'll park the car and walk over to practice afterwards. . . . It's mostly photographs, isn't it? Look at this picture of the 1930 Packers —everybody in street clothes, and look at the length of those overcoats. The Packers look like a bunch of hit men. Read that caption: 'They *merged* victories nine times" . . . you'd think they'd take more care. Actually, I found a word misspelled in my NFL contract this year. Hey! You hear that voice? That's Lombardi's voice. They must have a film going in here somewhere. 'What the hell's going on out there!' That's him, all right. That was a favorite line. 'What the hell's going on out there!' Angry as a hornet he is about something. Curious places, these football halls of fame. So little to put in them that gives a sense of the game. Dead men's voices . . . deflated footballs with the dates in white paint on them . . . old photographs . . . empty uniforms . . . ghostly places. The men just sucked out of those uniforms like vacuum cleaners had got to them. Look! There's a football I snapped in a championship game—1965. Actually had my hands around it. Preserved behind glass . . . think of that! There's another. Look, there are the pieces of wood they took out of Jerry Kramer—they'd been in him for years without his knowing. Fence splinters. He'd been thrown off a horse when he was a kid. Well, have we had enough of this? There's Lombardi's voice again. Let's go on out to the practice field.

"Look! The teams are out there. There wasn't that big fence around the field then. I bet that's going to cut off a lot of the breeze. Maybe not. The wind just whips in off the lake, steady, and nothing's going to cut it. There are the crowds standing there off Oneida Avenue. We used to get tremendous crowds here to watch practice. Very strange feeling, looking out over the practice field; it's very much like going back to your old grammar school or your old high school. It used to seem so much bigger. I wonder how much of my perspiration is out in that soil. Gallons. I know every blade of grass out there. Centers are the only players who look down . . . we see little creatures and things whisking around in the grass, doing whatever they do. I find flowers. I put them in my belt buckle. Or if it's hot, I pull out a long blade of grass and put it in my mouth. I've found a bit of money. It's strange to scrimmage with a nickel in your hand, because there's no pocket you can slide it into, and you wouldn't dare give it to a coach.

There was a tower right in the middle of the field. Lombardi liked to stand up on it, especially on Fridays, when he'd watch the screen passes, and the blocking downfield develop. I'd hear his voice coming out of the sky: 'Wider, Curry!' or 'Too quick, Curry!' One day the tower toppled over and fell on Ray Nitschke's head. He had his headgear on or the tower would have finished him. He took it off and threw it to the equipment manager. 'Gimme another!' It had a hole where a bolt had almost gone through. Lombardi wasn't on the tower when it went over. Some of the guys thought that was too bad. There were six bottles of water under the tower, but you weren't allowed to drink out of them. I don't know why they were there —to look at, I guess—though one time I remember Max McGee snuck in there without Lombardi seeing him and he guzzled down about three of them. He smacked his lips and he said, 'The stuff's damn good even with*out* Scotch in it!'

Look, it's beginning to rain. The umbrellas are going up; the people will stay and watch. They'd stay and watch through a bunch of waterspouts. The offense still wears green and defense white. It varies from team to team. In Baltimore the offense wore white and defense wore blue. In L.A., offense wore white, defense blue. At Houston we all wore white, which is why we couldn't tell the difference from one another! There they are, the yellow helmets and the *G* for Green Bay. That white-headed fellow is Tom Miller, who's one of the guys that signed me. Wait a minute. No, it isn't. That's not Tom—I don't know who that is. I'll tell you . . . I don't want to get too close . . . be recognized. I'd as soon stay back here. . . . I can't help remembering that Lombardi had three days of practice for the rookies before the veterans came in, but if he heard a veteran was in town he'd go crazy to think he was there without being down on the practice field *working.* He'd scour the town for him. That happened to Willie Davis once. He came to town early to get himself settled in . . . but Lombardi heard about it and thought of him as 'sneaking around shirking work' and the coaches were sent out to collar him. So at Green Bay the veterans turned up about seven minutes before the deadline.

"Look. You can see Bart Starr there with the green golfing cap. He'll be a fine coach. Perfect gentleman. Reeker of competence. So thorough and attentive.

"I wonder if he'll let me drive my car back and forth to practice. I suspect we'll all have to ride in the yellow school buses. You got to have them for the guys who don't have a car . . . the rookies coming in like I did ten years ago. They bridge the gap, don't they, those old yellow school buses?

"Very strange feeling. I'll feel better when I start putting on my shoulder pads and stuff . . . the things that I hate, but they are so familiar and common to the trade, no matter where you go, and it brings everything back to a common denominator.

"Being part of a team has so much to do with it. Football is very impersonal in terms of the adversary. I never used to look at the faces . . . just a helmet and a number across the line. So I didn't think too much about them. But now, more and more, I have found myself in the last two years looking into the guy's eyes to try to see what he's feeling, or what he's thinking. Is he afraid out here? It's not just to seek a tactical advantage. It's really, finally, to see what kind of person he is . . . almost as if I were looking in a mirror to try to find out what sort of a person *I* am."

Afterword

I shut off the recorder and went back to New York. We kept in touch. Bill Curry did not last out the training season. His hamstring injury continued to slow him, and in the last week of July Bart Starr called him in to say that the two young centers in camp would fight it out for the starting position. Curry was spared the indignity of being asked to bring in his playbook. The two old friends talked easily. Starr wanted him to stay in the Packer organization. Curry said he would think about it; he spent the remainder of his Packer contract scouting colleges for the draft as he wondered what he wanted to do next.

Some of his friends hoped he might try something else—clear out of football. His contacts were extensive, and opportunities many . . . television, business, politics.

But perhaps it was inevitable that the tug of the sport was too strong. In the spring of 1976, Curry accepted a job as an assistant coach at his alma mater, Georgia Tech—returning full circle even further back in time than Green Bay.

Quitting active football was not as hard as he imagined it had been for a man like Ray Nitschke. But it had been a closing out, a frightening sense of cessation, and when he first told me about it over the phone I remembered Dylan Thomas's line "After the first death there is no other."

Yes, Bill had said. He thought that was an appropriate enough sentiment.

Then in January, 1977, Bart Starr phoned Curry at his Atlanta home and offered him the offensive line coach job with the Packers. Curry spent a day thinking about the offer, talking it over with his wife, Carolyn, and then he called Starr back and said he was accepting. He hung up the phone, and he thought of the long trip north, that same route we had taken, and that he had another July to look forward to.